*Melissa's Journey
Standing in Freedom
A story of God's Love
By Melissa Fisher*

Dedication

I would like to express my deepest gratitude to my Father, God, who is the inspiration behind every word written on these pages. Without Him, my story would be incomplete, for He is not only the author, but also the finisher of my journey. Through His guidance, I have witnessed the impossible becoming possible. I am forever grateful for His unwavering love and support. I have been blessed with the opportunity to know God on an intimate level. Through the ups and downs, the triumphs and failures, I have come to experience His presence in my life. He has been my constant companion, guiding me through the darkest times. This book is a testament to His faithfulness and a tribute to the transformative power of His love in and through my life.

Table of Contents

Chapter 1 Page 5 The birth of a beautiful baby girl

Chapter 2 Page 39 Letting go

Chapter 3 Page 63 Taking a leap of faith

Chapter 4 Page 95 A new found love

Chapter 5 Page 123 Facing Life or Death

Chapter 6 Page 143 Change unfolds

Chapter 7 Page 169 An encounter with demons

Chapter 8 Page 191 Fighting my way to peace

Chapter 9 Page 217 Standing in Freedom

Introduction

As I gain traction on this road to freedom, I face obstacles that test my faith. Even though these roadblocks seem daunting, they will serve as opportunities for personal growth. As I attempt to overcome these obstacles, I seem weak at first. Because of these trials, I will develop strength and fortification within myself. As I make my way through the turbulent waters of life, each breath takes me deeper into the sea of defeat. Gasping for air, my heart beats against the currents of this world. During this moment, it is easy to lose sight of what truly matters. Though I face the temptation to drift from my purpose, I hold on, pursuing every answer my heart yearns for. Despite setbacks and uncertainties, I can't let them deter me. The journey may be long and winding, but through these challenges, I am strengthened. The weight of the world continuously threatens to consume me. With every breath, I take one step forward. As I walk, my eyes are met with obstacles on my way to freedom.

Chapter 1

The birth of a beautiful baby girl

After many years of anticipation, the day has finally come! Mom's dream has come true! On July 9, 1982, at 9 p.m., my presence is welcomed into the world. The breath of life consumes me, and while so tiny and precious, I crave warmth and love. The entire family surrounds me with joy never seen before. My overwhelming presence brings mom to tears as she stares into my beautiful brown eyes. My entire family's heart overflows with happiness as they cherish this moment. From that very first day, my mom's love for me is evident. The bond between a mother and a child is unbreakable. I am the only girl in my family. I hold a special place among my six brothers as a middle child. Mom has always dreamed of having a large family. She is determined to create a loving, supportive home filled with laughter and joy. From crawling to walking, I must learn to adapt to the world around me. One of my first memories happened at the age of five. Until this moment, I had no worries or knowledge of my existence. In December of 1987, with winter here, there are many things to look forward to. Christmas is the most significant holiday for my family. Mom has always taught us that Santa Claus will visit us if we stay well-behaved throughout the year.

So, all year round I strive to be on my best behavior. I hope to wake up on Christmas morning to find lots of presents under the beautiful tree. However, this year, my desires are much different. Only time will reveal whether my dreams will come to pass. As I eagerly anticipate Christmas, I want a few specific items. First and foremost, I long for a Barbie doll. With her stunning outfits, flowing hair, and endless imagination, Barbie will bring me hours of joy and companionship. The mere thought of making countless adventures and dressing her up in various ensembles fills me with excitement. Furthermore, I desire to acquire a Barbie house. Thinking of a miniature place where she can relax, entertain friends, and make memories, sparks my imagination. The idea of arranging furniture, designing the interior, and watching Barbie's world come to life is intriguing. Lastly, I yearn for a cabbage patch doll. These adorable, soft-bodied dolls with distinct faces and yarn hair have captured my attention. The thought of nurturing and caring for a cabbage patch doll, like a real baby, fills me with tenderness. As the holiday season approaches, I eagerly await Christmas morning. Will Santa Claus grant my wishes? As my mind wanders, I'm left filled with hope and anticipation. The presence of lights, ornaments, and the delightful aroma of pine creates an unparalleled experience.

The holiday season brings an enchanting atmosphere filled with excitement. The twinkling lights create a magical ambiance, while the ornaments add a touch of charm to the Christmas tree. The scent of pine fills the air, evoking memories of past celebrations and warming my heart. The holiday spirit brings a sense of peace and happiness that is indescribable. It is a time when worries fade, and the focus shifts to love, family, and gratitude. But, as the days pass, my anxiety runs rampant. As I try to embrace this time, deep breaths ease my thoughts. The time has come, faster than I ever perceived. Christmas Eve has arrived, and sleep is nowhere in sight. The anticipation makes it impossible for me to rest. All I want to do is stay awake, hoping to glimpse

Santa Claus. The thought of Christmas firsthand fills me with a childlike wonder. My mind wanders as I lay there. I reflect on the true meaning of Christmas. The gifts and material possessions become secondary to the love and connection shared during this special time of year. It is a time to appreciate the blessings in life and spread kindness and joy to others.

I am at rest knowing that Christmas morning will soon come. And so, with a heart filled with thankfulness, I drift off to sleep. The following day, as the sun gently peeks through my window, I am filled with many emotions. I jump out of bed and rush into the living room as my heart pounds with anticipation. To my delight, a treasure trove of presents awaits me underneath the tree! As my eyes open, I'm filled with excitement. With my feet barely touching the ground, I rush to the pile of gifts. But just as I am about to reach out and grab one, mom stops me in my tracks. Her voice gently reminds me to eat breakfast before opening any presents. The words hang in the air, momentarily dampening my enthusiasm. I know she means well, but these few minutes will feel like an eternity. With my eyes fixated on the presents, I embrace the sweet smell of freshly cooked pancakes. As I take bites, I barely notice the taste of the delicious pancakes.

Upon finishing my breakfast, I jump up from my seat and dash toward the Christmas tree. With my hands trembling, I carefully select the first present and unwrap it. The wrapping paper tears away and reveals a brand-new toy. A surge of delight envelops me as I acknowledge the manifestation of my long-held desires. The excitement builds as I move on to the next and then, the next. One by one, the presents reveal themselves, bringing me closer to pure happiness. The addition of these lovely gifts has brought me so much joy. I've been blessed with a Barbie, a Barbie house, a cabbage patch, and a Mr. Potato Head. Not to mention the magical moments that my family makes. So with a heart full of thankfulness, I take a moment to appreciate my blessings. I feel truly fortunate to have such a wonderful family in my life. I desperately want to fit in with everyone, especially my brothers. It's imperative for me to feel like I belong.

However, there are many things I have to grow accustomed to. At just five years old, there's still so much I don't quite understand. However, I'm trying to learn the importance of patience. So, as I shake off the unknowns, I rest in finding my place in life. But just as quickly as happiness came, it quickly dissipates.

In a matter of months, the first attack on my life comes like a thief in the night. On January 20, 1987, mom makes a quick but smart decision while stumbling upon a broken water heater. She decides to heat water on the stove to bathe before work. Once the water is poured into the pot, she sets the timer and waits. While she waits, my oldest brother Jordan grabs the pot and heads to the bathroom. But before he could make it, we bump into each other. It happens so quickly, leaving me little to no time to react. Before I realize what is happening, my body becomes saturated with boiling water. The scalding liquid engulfs me, causing unimaginable pain. The shock is overwhelming, and I can't help but let out a piercing scream. Immediately, I collapse into the floor, wrestling with agony. The pain intensifies with each passing second, and I desperately kick my legs in an attempt to find relief.

Seeing the anguish in my eyes, Mom rushes to my side. She gently lifts me off the floor and carries me to the bathroom. My skin clings to the fabric as mom carefully removes my shirt, causing even more excruciating pain. The realization sinks in that the burn is severe, and immediate medical attention is needed. With a calm demeanor, mom grabs cold towels from the linen closet and places them on the affected area. The coldness soothes the burning sensation, although it's only temporary. The fear of the long-term consequences lingers in the back of my mind. While comforting me, we anxiously await the ambulance's arrival. In this time of crisis, every second feels like an eternity. I cling to any source of comfort, desperately trying to find relief. The agonizing moments pass by slowly, each one more unbearable than the last. With time passing, the pain intensifies, losing control of my senses. I feel my consciousness fading. During this terrifying ordeal, mom stands strong by my side, providing me with the support I need.

Her presence alone brings a sense of stability and reassurance in this chaotic situation. As the EMT arrives they see that because of severity of my injury, a helicopter is needed. I must be life-flighted to Shriners in Galveston, Texas.

As the sound of the approaching helicopter pierces through the air, it offers me a glimmer of hope amidst my despair. The EMTs carefully transfer me onto the aircraft, taking every precaution to minimize the pain. The helicopter propels into the sky, its roar drowning out the world below. Inside, the EMT administers pain medicine, providing me with some much-needed relief. The medication takes effect, dulling the intensity of the burning sensation. At this critical moment, my life hangs in the balance. As time passes my arrival at the hospital comes quickly. Upon entering the hospital I find comfort, knowing that things will be okay. The skilled doctors at Shriners work tirelessly to save me. Their expertise and dedication give me hope. Due to this horrific incident, I have suffered extensive third-degree burns on my chest and a portion of my neck. The physical pain is unbearable, but the emotional toll it has taken is equally troublesome. As I lay here in the hospital, a sense of insecurity creeps in. In these difficult moments, I am reminded of the importance of holding myself together. I must find the strength to face this adversity head-on. It is a constant battle to maintain a positive mindset. The hospital environment can be a lonely place, filled with uncertainty and fear. But I must rely on my inner resilience and determination.

I refuse to let this incident define me or control my emotions. I am determined to rise above the pain and sadness that threaten my life. Every day is a new challenge, both physically and emotionally. The healing process is slow and painful, but I am committed to stay on course. I draw strength from the support of my loved ones, who remind me that I am not alone. The road to recovery may be long and difficult but I refuse to let it break me. As long as I have the will to survive, I know that good things will come, even though this moment may feel overwhelming. I am young and haven't had the chance to experience many things yet. Deep down, I know that there is more to life. It is through these difficult moments that my understanding of life becomes clearer. While I can't comprehend why this hardship is happening, I know that there is a purpose. Perhaps it's meant to shape me into a better version of myself, to teach me valuable lessons, or to prepare me for the future. Despite the questions, I am determined to keep pushing through, knowing there are brighter days ahead.

Life may throw curveballs at me, but I am confident that I have the strength to navigate through them. On this journey, starting with this trauma, I come to appreciate the small victories. They serve as reminders that even in hardship, there is still goodness to be found. It is important to cherish these moments and hold onto them. I want to explore the world and discover its wonders. I want to learn from different cultures, and meet new people, and broaden my horizons. There is a whole world out there waiting to be explored. Though I may face uncertainty, I am confident that this journey will lead to a place of fulfillment and happiness. I want to make the most out of this life and leave a positive impact on the world. I believe that by staying true to myself and following my passions, I will find the answers I seek and the purpose I long for. So, as I navigate this winding road, I hold onto my will to survive. I may not have all the answers now, but I will continue seeking them. I know that I need to heal properly, but the days seem to be going by so slowly. The skin grafts and surgeries are taking their toll on my emotional and physical state. Before I can leave the hospital, I must undergo a fitting for a burn suit. Medical professionals have emphasized the significance of this procedure as it will greatly contribute to my recovery.

The time I will need to wear this suit is determined by how well my wounds heal. The maximum time I may have to wear it could extend up to a year. Even while the future may be scary this is something I must endure. From the very first moment I put on the burn suit, I can't help but notice the discomfort. Wearing this suit will bring about a subtle yet significant transformation, although its impact may not be immediately apparent. It requires exerting pressure on the burn area, which serves as a crucial step in my recovery. Gradually, I will begin to comprehend and internalize my altered appearance. However, I refuse to allow this change to hinder my progress. Instead, I embrace the new version of myself. With no choice but to hold on, I take a deep breath and continue fighting. From the initial shock of the accident to the pain of the surgeries, each day has been a test of my endurance. The constant worry and the fear of the unknown have weighed heavily on my soul. So, I take each day as it comes, focusing on the small things and finding gratitude during this situation. I lean on the support of my loved ones and the guidance of the medical professionals who are overseeing my treatment. I trust their expertise and know they have my best interests at heart.

After a month of undergoing treatment, it's finally time to leave. This past month has come and gone so fast. I can hardly grasp where the time has gone. I know I have a long road ahead. Once I return home, all I want is to be alone. The weight of my emotions becomes too much to handle in the presence of others. In the solitude, I find solace, a refuge from the chaos surrounding me.

The tears come unbidden, almost every night, as I yearn to free myself from the clutches of this painful memory. It haunts my every thought, like a ghostly presence that refuses to fade away. The person I once was feels like a distant memory, a fragment of a past life. I try to accept that this is the new me, but it's a concept that eludes my senses. It's difficult to grasp the idea that I am forever changed. It will take time to understand that the person I used to be is gone. At times, it feels as if I'm trapped in a never-ending nightmare, waiting for the moment when I will wake up. But that moment never comes, and I'm left to navigate through the darkness of my mind. The emotions that rush through my head sometimes, are incomprehensible. I need to get a grip on things and find my balance.

I'm too young to have to deal with so much, but I have no say in the matter. The more I think about what has happened, the harder it becomes to find peace. Sleep has always been my refuge. A sanctuary where I can escape from the harsh realities of life. It's in the quiet stillness of the night that I could find a momentary respite from the weight of my troubles. Trying to remember how things were before the accident, I lay there in an attempt to rest. Being surrounded by the familiar comfort of my pillows and blankets, I can feel the tension slowly dissipating. But there are nights when sleep eludes me when the pain becomes overbearing. It is during these moments that I find myself staring at the ceiling, lost in a swirl of emotions. The thoughts and worries that plague my mind grow stronger with each passing second, making it almost impossible to find rest. As I toss and turn, I am determined to find my balance. The nightmares of that tragic moment haunt me relentlessly, leaving me waking up in a cold sweat. The memories are etched into my mind, replaying like a horror movie on an endless loop. Each night, I find myself grappling with the fear and anxiety that stems from that fateful night.

However, I have found a way to face this new version of myself that emerged from the darkness. My goal is to overcome this unfamiliar territory with courage. But the more I try to confront my fears, the deeper I sink into the sea of despair.

Throughout the year, I have been plagued by a constant sense of dread. Every day feels like an uphill battle as if I am wading through quicksand, struggling to find solid ground. The weight of burdens becomes heavier with time, making it increasingly challenging to seek comfort. To make matters worse, I have been left to wear this horrific suit for an entire year. Despite the overwhelming darkness that surrounds me, a glimmer of happiness arises from within. I realize that the time has come for me to shed this suffocating suit off my tiny body. I can feel butterflies fluttering in my tummy, mixed with anticipation and nervousness. I've been preparing myself to break free from this stifling discomfort for such a long time. Dealing with the scars left by that haunting night will require perseverance, and a willingness to confront the demons within. I am ready for the battle that lies ahead, ready to face the unknown.

With a sense of relief, the suffocating, tight-fitting feeling has been removed. It is liberating to be free from discomfort. I can finally breathe without any restraint, and it's like a weight has been lifted off my shoulders. As the initial relief fades away, a hint of hesitation creeps in. I find myself standing in front of the mirror, unsure of what I will see. For days I pace back and forth in front of the mirror. But the curiosity gets overwhelming, and I can't resist the urge to take a peek. Slowly, as I turn my gaze toward the mirror, my heart begins to race. What I encounter in the mirror shocks me to the core. A cruel illusion has been cast upon my skin. It looks as if someone has taken plastic and meticulously embedded it into my flesh, leaving behind a deep scar. The sight is so unbearable that I can't help but drop to the floor. In shock, I find myself crying uncontrollably. The reality of this horrific scar becomes too much to bear. The thought of exposing it to anyone fills me with embarrassment. As I grow anxious, all I want is to live in isolation. The scar serves as a constant reminder of the pain I endured. It's a visible mark that tells a story of struggle and adversity. I wish I could hide it away and pretend it doesn't exist, but the reality is undeniable. As I pick myself up from the floor, I realize that this scar is now a part of me. It may be a permanent reminder of a difficult situation, but it also represents resilience and strength. I may hesitate to show it to others, but deep down, I know that it's a testament to overcoming difficulties. I don't want anyone to make fun of me, so turtlenecks become a part of my new wardrobe. Coming to grips with my new look gives me the drive I need to jump over this hurdle. The world around me can sometimes make it hard to be confident. The turtle necks serve as a shield, protecting me from the judgment of others. Each day, I am reminded that it is not about what others think of me, but rather how I feel about myself. I am grateful for the lessons and the growth that comes from overcoming this trauma. I place my mind on more positive moments so I ask mom if we can do some outdoor activities. Before I was burned mom loved taking us fishing and swimming. In the past, we often did many outdoor activities.

    This past year, I've been forced to stay away from some things that I love. So mom decides to take us to the creek for a fishing trip. With the beautiful weather ahead the sun shines bright and the air is filled with warmth. As we make our way to the creek, a sense of excitement and joy fills my heart. I can't help but wear the biggest smile on my face. Being back in the water, surrounded by nature's beauty, is even better than I could have imagined. There is serenity and peace found in the presence of water. Mom has told me stories of when I was a baby, and how she always has a hard time keeping me away from it. The gentle sound of the flowing creek and the shimmering reflections on the surface create a tranquil atmosphere. In these moments, all the worries and troubles seem to fade away. The trauma that had once threatened to take my joy is no match for the peace I'm experiencing. As I swim in the creek, I am overtaken by a renewed sense of energy. There is nothing that can ever take the place of these memories.

With happiness being reunited from within my soul things will only keep getting brighter. Approximately eighteen months into my recovery, mom makes a significant decision for our family. She decides to bring a cat into our lives. Love immediately set in the moment I lay my eyes on her. I must give her the perfect name.

After a few days, I settle on the name Cheshire. Little did I know at the time, having Cheshire around would prove to be immensely beneficial for me in my emotional battles. The mere presence of Cheshire brings me a sense of comfort that I never anticipated. Her playful antics and gentle nature have had a profound impact on me. She brings a smile to my face that permeates our home. It's as if her presence alone is a serenade of peace, providing balance to my surroundings. With each passing day, my bond with Cheshire grows. I find myself spending more and more time with her, cherishing the moments we share. She becomes a loyal confidant who listens without judgment. Recognizing the positive influence Cheshire has on me, my mother graciously allows her to sleep in my room. This simple act of accommodation further strengthens our connection.

As I wake up each morning I'm welcomed by her presence and gentle purring. It's as if she understands my struggles and offers her unwavering support in return. But one evening, mom tells me to sleep with her. So I place Cheshire in my closet and head to bed with mom. In the middle of the night, I'm startled by the smell of smoke. Mom wakes me up, demanding me to rush outside. With no time to think all I can do is vacate our home. Upon exiting the front door, I cry out in sadness begging mom to let me get Cheshire. But mom says it's too dangerous to go back in the house. The smoke is so intense, that the possibility of evacuating Cheshire is impossible. For the first time in my life, I've been able to experience the love of an animal. But the devastation of losing her hurts me intensely. As I sit down in the grass, I stare into the dark, filled with overwhelming sadness. My heart aches knowing Cheshire is trapped in the ruins of our house. Her innocent face flashes before my eyes, and I can't help but feel a sense of helplessness. The bond we shared was something special, and losing her felt like a dagger through my heart. I can still remember the first time I laid eyes on her precious face. There was a vulnerability in her eyes that drew me in. Cheshire's purrs were like music to my ears and brought endless laughter into my life.

She had become a part of my family, filling my days with unconditional love. Now, all those precious memories are saturated in smoke. The reality of the situation hits me like a ton of bricks. The pain is incomprehensible, and I can't help but question why such tragedy has fallen upon my life. The darkness of the night mirrors the pain in my heart. It's a pain that words cannot express, a loss that cuts deep into my heart. But amidst the devastation, I find joy in the memories of Cheshire that brought me happiness. The love we shared was real and will forever be cherished. But as I look up, in hopes that somehow, someday, healing will come. Time doesn't stand still and in the Summer of 1989, mom finds us a new home located on FM 1952. It is a cute little country-style home located in Wallis, TX, which is about thirty minutes from the home we lost in the fire. What makes this place truly remarkable is the enormous cornfield and the vast amount of land surrounding the property. From the moment I lay my eyes on it, I am filled with awe and wonder. As I stand there, gazing at the property, my mind is flooded with incredible visions. I imagine all the possibilities that this place holds for me.

The dream of having animals again fills me with great joy. I envision chickens and many other animals roaming freely around the yard. Finally, as we begin the process of moving into our new home, I feel a sense of contentment. Between packing and unpacking, the move seems endless. Like the house, my heart finds a place to call its own. I'm starting new, and with each passing day, our new home becomes a place of comfort. But with mom having to work long hours to provide for us, my brother Jordan is often left in charge. One bright early morning, after mom heads out for work, I decide to straighten up and unpack the rest of my boxes. While unpacking, I hear a knock at my door. As I turn my head towards the entrance, a sense of apprehension fills my heart. As I approach the door, I slowly open it. It's my oldest brother Jordan. Before I have the chance to ask him what he needs, he pries his way in and closes the door. I can't understand what he needs, so I ask him to leave. However, he refuses and demands that I lay on the bed and remain quiet. I feel a sense of fear and helplessness as he begins to stack boxes up against the door, trapping me inside.

My heart pounds in my chest as he starts to sexually abuse me. I am overwhelmed with confusion and disbelief, unable to comprehend the whole scenario. The violation of my body leaves me torn, and deeply violated. As tears well up in my eyes, he puts his hand over my mouth to silence my cries. He tells me to not say a word to anyone and if I do, no one will believe me. I'm emotionally trapped so I do just as he asks. I'm finding it very difficult to fully process the situation. I know deep down that what he is doing is wrong, but what can I do? Immediately following the first day of assault, I begin feeling different. My fear intensifies from within and I start to isolate myself. When mom returns, I try to not be suspicious. As hard as it is, while not wanting Jordan to hurt me, I stay quiet. The agony and shame are also settling in and I don't know what to do. Crying inside, I hope that this is the last time. But the next day, Jordan takes charge and instructs my brothers to go outside and play.

However, instead of joining them, he focuses his attention on me again.

Why is he doing this to me? I am subjected to sexual abuse for the second time. It is deeply distressing to know that Jordan is placed in charge every time my mom leaves. Knowing this, I now wonder how much longer I will have to be subjected to his abuse. I'm so stressed because there is no telling how long this will continue. Days go by, and the abuse persists daily. It is becoming a horrifying routine. Jordan is taking advantage of his position of authority whenever my mom is away. Six long days pass, and I am still trapped in this nightmare. Often I wonder when this torment will come to an end. Little to my surprise, there is a moment of hope arising in the sky. On the seventh day of this awful abuse, something unexpected happens. Once again, my brothers head outside to play. They are unaware of the darkness that lurks within our home. As they joyfully immerse themselves in their games, Jordan seizes the opportunity to lock the house door. I am isolated from the outside world. Locked in, I feel a mixture of panic and resignation. The walls of the house close in on me, mirroring the suffocating grip that Jordan has left on my life. I am left alone with my thoughts, my pain, and the realization that my safety and well-being are at the mercy of my abuser.

In this harrowing moment, I yearn for someone to rescue me from this confinement. The weight of my trauma becomes, even more, unbearable as I contemplate what lies ahead. The uncertainty looms over me, casting a shadow on any possibility of hope. But as I lie beneath the weight of his body, a sudden honk pierces the air, instantly jolting him off of me. Astonished by the fact that my mother has returned home early, I run outside with tears flowing down my cheeks. Unsure of what has emboldened me, a surge of energy races through my veins. Determined to no longer tolerate this abuse, I cry out in desperation, pleading with my mother to listen. However, she fails to grasp the gravity of the situation, overlooking my cry for help. From that very second I started to believe what Jordan said. The fact that my mom doesn't believe me places me deeper into isolation. Because of this trauma, rejection starts to rear its ugly head and loneliness overtakes my every thought. The pain inflicted on me has left deep scars, making it difficult for me to trust others. The reminder of being raped by my brother at the age of seven is life-changing. One thing I can't see coming is the impact this event will have on the rest of my life.

An uncomfortable uneasiness lingers in the air. What should be a haven has now been violated and turned into a horrific place for me to reside. With every day that passes, the more I feel trapped by fear. The thought of being left alone terrifies me, and I fear that I may never find peace again. It's a constant battle between wanting to connect with others and the fear of being hurt. But I'm stuck in this cycle, unsure of what steps to take to break free from my broken body, mind, and soul. The wounds of the past have made it hard for me to believe in the goodness of people, and that there are individuals who won't cause me harm. It's a struggle to open up, to let someone in, fearing that they too might become an abuser. However, amidst this overwhelming fear, I find strength in my ability to be patient. I hold onto the hope that with time that the pain will lessen and heal will come. It's a slow process, one that requires immense courage and determination. Each day, I remind myself that the fear won't consume me forever and that there is a light at the end of this dark tunnel.

Yet, the burden weighs heavily on me. With each passing moment the will to live becomes harder to bear. I struggle to find a balance between the desire to live a fulfilling life and the fear that lingers within me. In times like these, I often think of Jordan, who once said, "No one would...". Though the road ahead may be long and hard, I refuse to let pain dictate my future. Loneliness may haunt me, but I hope to finding a sense of belonging. All due to this situation, I'm rethinking love, wondering if what Jordan has done is really what true love is. The feelings of shame and disgust challenge my reasons for living and I begin to blame myself. Even though I try to block out the memories, the thoughts never stop. It is disheartening to see that he has faced no consequences for his actions, leaving me to bear the burden of guilt. These feelings of shame and disgust have shaken the foundations of my existence, making me question the purpose of my life. Despite my best efforts to suppress the memories, they persistently haunt me. The thoughts of what transpired refuse to leave my mind, reminding me of the pain I have experienced. I'm trying so hard to surpass these meaningful hurts but the struggle is extremely intense.

What exacerbates this situation is the absence of positive reinforcement. Without any form of encouragement or support, the weight of the emotional turmoil becomes more overwhelming. The lack of validation and reassurance makes it challenging to navigate through this difficult phase. As a result, I am confronted with a profound sense of shame. The impact on my emotional well-being cannot be understated. My world has been shattered, leaving me to pick up the pieces. Due to the lack of resistance, my brokenness starts to escalate. My attitude begins to spiral out of control as if caught in a whirlwind of negative emotions. The mountains in my mind are growing taller, casting long shadows over the valleys of my thoughts. The once bright and vibrant landscapes of my inner world now seem to be shrouded in darkness.

Just as the physical storms outside grow heavier, the storms within me become even more intense. Filled with rain and despair, these storms drench my spirit and dampen my sense of contentment. I am consumed by a sea of bitterness, struggling to let go of the past.

Learning to keep my emotions hidden from the world, silence and isolation overshadow my heart. Leaning on myself teaches me how to let go, even during this storm. No longer wanting to focus on my issues, I can't help but notice that things at home are getting worse. One of the reasons for this shift is Jordan's behavior at school. He has started causing trouble, and if nothing changes, it will lead to devastation. It is a troubling situation that requires immediate intervention. As the months pass, the situation with Jordan isn't improving. Mom receives news that Jordan has started some trouble and has been arrested. Living in the same house with him after he raped me has been hard but now with him gone, maybe I will find my peace again. Now that he is gone, the anticipation of my father's return hangs heavy in the air. History has taught me that his arrival marks the end of any long-term peace. His volatile temper and the dark shadow of his past actions loom over our home. Despite my understanding of the complex dynamics at play, it is difficult to understand the love my mother holds for him.

Mom clings to the hope that things can work out. But, it will take two to build a harmonious relationship. He has barely stepped foot back in the house and the fights once again come to the surface. With mom and dad fighting it's hard to have any solitude. Many nights I lay awake, anticipating the idea of sleep. But one late evening, dad decides to strike mom pretty hard and causes her to bleed. The cops come and make him vacate the premises. With a sigh of relief, I take a deep breath. I'm not sure just how much more I can take so I place my mind on the beauty around me. Things start to look up as I find comfort, surrounded by the outdoors while I inhale the smell of the country's fresh breezes. By rearranging my focus, I find solace in spending time with the animals. One of my favorite pastimes is observing the lively interactions between our chickens, rabbits, dogs, and cats.

The playful commotion they create never fails to make me smile. Whenever I seek comfort or need a listening ear, I often gravitate toward our dog, Ruby. Something about her presence puts me at ease. It's as if she understands the weight of my thoughts and emotions. Ruby has become my new therapy.

I can't help but chuckle whenever I think of her. It's a whimsical reminder of the joy she brings. I find peace in venting my frustrations and worries to her. Though she may not respond in words, her gentle licks and warm gazes make me feel understood. It's as if she empathizes with my pain, that transcends beyond our language barriers. As tears of relief stream down my face, I find safety in her presence. In the midst of life's challenges, the bond I share with Ruby becomes a grounding force. The unconditional love and non-judgmental nature of our connection remind me that I deserve laughter. As I continue to navigate through life's ups and downs, I am grateful for the animals who have found their way into my heart. They all remind me to embrace the moment, find happiness within their company, and cherish the simple joys that life brings. In their unique ways, they all teach me the power of love, authenticity, and the healing nature of animal companionship. But even then, when will all this chaos become a thing of the past? Will I ever have a normal life? How many more times will I be hurt? How many more hurdles will I need to jump through?

Melissa's Journey " Standing in Freedom " 38

Chapter 2

Letting Go

In the Summer of 1991 after all of the chaos settles, my family decides to move back to East Bernard. Mom wants to steer away from the painful memories made on FM 1952, and so do I. The previous obstacles may have momentarily blocked my view, but I am embracing this opportunity for another start. This new place holds the potential to help me overcome the painful memories from my past that haunt me. We have a diverse household, a mix of animals, each with unique charm and character. We have dogs, cats, rabbits, and chickens, and grows with the addition of three adorable horses. These quarter horses, the mom's name is Bonnie, Apple the daughter, and Spirit the son, become an unexpected part of my life. The road ahead is promising and it will bring immense joy and excitement. From the first glimpse, I immediately fall in love. They are magnificent creatures with sleek coats, gentle eyes, and graceful movements. I have been fortunate enough to witness my mom's interactions with them, and it is truly a sight to behold. They have a special connection built on trust, respect, and love. Words cannot describe just how beautiful these animals move.

It's amazing to see how my mom communicates with them effortlessly. It is a bond that goes beyond words, a language that they alone can understand. My mom's bond with Bonnie specifically reminds me so much of my relationship with Ruby. Her horse, Bonnie, has such a unique color. It looks as if someone took paint cans and threw them all over her coat. Bonnie is my mom's pride and joy. She rides Bonnie almost every day. To watch the way Bonnie runs is truly captivating. The graceful movement of her strong legs and the wind blowing through her mane create a mesmerizing sight. My mom's gentle touch and Bonnie's responsive nature make their partnership a true joy to observe. Watching them, I take mental notes, learning how to groom Bonnie, feed her, and ensure her well-being. I eagerly anticipate the day when I'll be able to ride Bonnie, Apple or even Spirit. Never in my wildest dreams could I have imagined this part of my journey. I am so grateful for the unexpected blessings that have come my way and I can't wait to see what new opportunities await me in the future. I am excited to learn how to take care of horses and maybe one day ride them. But for now, I learn from watching my mom. This whole time I've been using the love of the horses as a way to escape from my pain.

While I try to overlook my deep pain, it hurts to ignore these scars I carry. By embracing this love for the horses, I find myself at ease. But Ruby, our blue heeler, keeps the most special place in my heart. One day as I gaze upon her, I notice something wrong. So, I call mom to come and take a look at her. It seems as if she has been chewing on her jaw. She investigates and finds that Ruby has been kicked by one of the horses. She is a cattle dog and would often chase the horses so this doesn't come as a surprise. After contemplating, mom is left with no choice but to put her down. So my brothers take me away so the adults can handle the issue. I am too young to understand all that is happening but I knew that Ruby is hurt badly. When I come home and see that she is no longer here, I knew she was gone. It's so hard to deal with so much pain and losing Ruby hits me like an eighteen-wheeler, head-on. She has been my counselor and friend. When I needed to talk, she listened. But now that she is gone, I feel so lost.

With all this unnecessary chaos circling, rest is what I truly need. No matter how precious I think the horses are, I still can't seem to overcome my scars. The feeling of emptiness lingers in my chest, and I struggle to understand what is causing this profound sense of longing. It's as if a dark cloud has settled over my heart, leaving it stained with sorrow. Despite my best efforts to ignore the wounds buried deep within, they persistently remind me of their existence. The pain cannot be silenced forever. And in the depths of my being, there is a flicker of hope that refuses to fade away. The dream of finding happiness ignites a fire within me, urging me to fight against the odds. Just when it seems like I am teetering on the edge of breaking, life's tumultuous waves pull me further into the abyss. Lost at sea, the vastness of the unknown, causes my will to survive to waver. My heart bears the weight of its scars, etched into its very core. The stains run deep, reminding me of the battles fought and the wounds suffered. It is a constant reminder of the strength it takes to carry on, even when the burdens seem insurmountable. In this state of emotional turmoil, I search for guidance and understanding. I yearn to find the missing piece that will wash away the stains and restore my heart to its true essence. Until then, I continue to sail through the treacherous waters, holding onto hope. No matter how hard I fight, there is darkness in the corner of my mind that refuses to leave.

But I try my best to see the light in the dark. Looking ahead, I place my pain deep within my head where it's hard to reach. As I begin the fifth grade, I am determined to break free from my reserved nature. I decided to immerse myself in child-like activities. It is during this time that my teacher approaches me with an exciting opportunity to join a square dance skit. Without hesitation, I accept the invitation. From the very first day of practice, I sense this is something meant for me. The lively music, the synchronized movements, and the cheerful atmosphere captivate me. As the days go by and practice intensifies, my passion for square dancing grows. I find myself yearning to do more, to perfect each step, and to become a true performer. The skit not only allows me to step out of my comfort zone but also provides me with newfound confidence. Through countless hours of practice, I learn the importance of teamwork and discipline.

Each day, I eagerly look forward to the dance rehearsals, cherishing the moments of joy and camaraderie shared with my fellow dancers. As the school year progresses, the day of the performance finally arrives. Excitement fills the air as I take my position on the stage. The spotlight shines upon me, and the audience eagerly awaits the performance. I feel a surge of exhilaration, knowing that I have overcome my inhibitions, embracing this opportunity. The square dance not only showcases my newfound talent but also serves as a reminder of the incredible growth I have achieved. It symbolizes my willingness to explore new horizons, take risks, and embrace the unknown. The applause from the audience validated my efforts. With every beat, I feel a surge of determination. I'm reminded that dreams should be pursued, no matter how big or small. As I'm fueled by my love for dance, a burning desire to share my talent with the world conspires. I start taking an interest in much more than just dance skits. My vision shifts to hip-hop dance. While watching others on television I decided to embrace a new endeavor. The dream of choreographing hip-hop dance becomes more tangible.

I start experimenting with different styles, exploring new ways to express myself through movement. I am set on pursuing my dream, and to continue growing as a dancer. In the end, it doesn't matter if I ever make it onto a show like Star Search or achieve fame and recognition. What matters is the joy I find in dancing and the therapeutic release it provides. So, I will keep dancing, keep creating, and keep dreaming. Because in the world of dance, anything is possible. With every beat and every step, I am one step closer to realizing my potential and fulfilling my passion. Maybe one day my dream of being a choreographer will happen, so I hold onto my vision. But even if I don't, it's an amazing thing to have found the skill of dance and peace in my life. And even while dancing continues to be a place in my heart, my focus shifts toward other desires. I yearn to discover my true identity and unravel the depths of my inner being. Reading captivates my attention, and the library becomes my new sanctuary. I may have just found my comfort in the world of books where I can seek inspiration and guidance.

Each word resonates with my soul, allowing me to explore various perspectives, and gain a deeper understanding of myself.

As my passion for reading becomes evident, my teacher takes notice of my enthusiasm. Recognizing my eagerness to express myself creatively, she suggests that I channel my energy into a new skit. It becomes a platform for me to learn the unique interpretation of the characters and storylines from books. As I choose a book, I delve into different genres and narratives. While rehearsing characters are brought to life. Through this collaborative effort, I appreciate diverse perspectives and empathy toward others.

Making the skit becomes a transformative experience. It ignites my imagination and fuels my creativity. As I immerse myself in the world of books, I discover hidden talents thus unleashing my full potential. The lesson becomes a testament to my growth. It showcases my ability to adapt, collaborate, and bring stories to life. Though a future of being a choreographer lingers in the corner of my mind, the journey of self-discovery has opened new doors of possibility. The past few years have been a test of endurance and perseverance, and I'm proud of the progress I've made. After a long yet promising year, the summer is right around the corner.

I've accomplished so much this year and learned so much more about myself. And because of my hard work and dedication at school, I receive a beautiful watch at my fifth-grade graduation. From the moment I lay my eyes on the watch, I'm captivated by its sheer beauty. It's truly astonishing! The watch is undoubtedly the most exquisite piece of jewelry, carefully crafted to perfection. The watch features a sleek black leather strap that adds a touch of elegance to its design. It feels smooth against my skin and complements any outfit I wear. The gold bezel surrounding the watch face adds a touch of luxury and sophistication. As its shimmering hue catches the light, it becomes even more eye-catching. What makes this watch special is the Brahma imprinted inside the case. The Brahma is our school's beloved mascot, and its presence on the watch serves as a constant reminder of the memories I hold on to from school.

The watch creates memories for me of my efforts, reminding me that dedication and perseverance have paid off.

Tears well up in my eyes as I reflect on my accomplishments. Some moments drown out my pain but completely shaking my past off seems impossible. The fear of being judged and misunderstood renders me silent, keeping my trauma hidden from those who are close. They have no idea of the pain and struggles that lurk behind my eyes. But, the more I ignore my issue, the more it becomes haunting. Suppressing my emotions and refusing to confront my history is taking a toll on my mental well-being. It is a heavy burden that I carry alone, falsely believing that I can handle it without seeking support. But I've already been rejected once so why would anyone believe me now? Continually lying to myself about the impact of my past, I inadvertently harm my interactions with those around me. The unresolved pain and bitterness that I harbor inside seep into my actions and behavior.

 As a result, my relationships begin to suffer. The inability to address my past hinders my connection with others. My head spins out of control as the weight of my hidden history grows. Wages of an internal battle begin to spill over into my external world, exposing the cracks in the facade. Every part of my being is slipping right through my fingers. I'm desperately trying to hold onto everything intangible. While I try to cover up my internal scars, the more they continue to surface. The temporary fixes I seek only provide momentary relief, thus leaving the emptiness only to return. With each passing day, anger and bitterness continue to grow, consuming me from within. It's as if I'm climbing a staircase, each step feeling more challenging than the last. The weight of my heart's damage makes it hard to envision any hope in my future. Quite often mom would leave me at home with all of my brothers. Out of fear, I would lash out, hoping she would take me away with her. When she would not allow me to come, I began breaking windows. Slamming doors also become my new normal, in hopes of getting the attention I need. The wounds run deep, continuously leaving me broken and lost.

But amidst this darkness, I hold onto the hope that healing is coming. My whole life is in total ruin. I must keep searching for the light that guides me out of this, even if it feels impossibly far away. As the battle in my head continues, the struggle to fight for survival intensifies. As I navigate through the chaos, the weight of the world seems to be resting on my shoulders. Even in difficult times, I can't deny it's difficult to keep my head high. But as I come back to reality, I start to think about those things that make me happy. Food has always brought me happiness. Mom is an extraordinary cook and she often makes some amazing dishes. Among them all, homemade rice krispies are my favorite. These awesome treats bring comfort to my soul. With every bite, a small ray of sunshine begins to break through the thick clouds. It's in these little moments on my journey, that I find extraordinary comfort. The contentment is so enjoyable, even if it's only for a short while. If only I could escape the prison of my thoughts, then maybe there would be a chance for true liberation. Food and sweets help me when I'm down but I desire so much more.

 If sweets could erase all the pain that has distorted my thoughts then my happiness would inevitably run rampant. But the constant battle within my mind can be overwhelming, suffocating even. It's like being trapped in a never-ending loop of negativity and doubt. As I reflect on my past, I realize that the life I am living now is better than what it used to be. I have come a long way from where I started, and I refuse to let my past define me. Optimism is my guiding light, my anchor in the storm. I must keep going even when everything looks as if it's falling apart. The constant pull and tug of my emotions causes drastic and painful results. And things all around me are never calm for very long. So, as quickly as the sun comes out, it soon will leave. On one cold, rainy day, the fog grows so thick that it's hard to see my hand. I have never experienced this amount of fog in all my life. Despite the unfavorable weather, mom braves the elements and sets off on her way into town. While aware of the potential dangers that lie ahead, as she leaves, we exchange glances. With each passing minute that she doesn't return, worry grows. The whole family begins to question her whereabouts.

Why hasn't she made it back yet? Anxiously checking the clock, we find ourselves hoping for her safe return. With the rain pouring down relentlessly and the fog becoming even denser, the weather worsens. But as we begin to fear the worst, a flicker of light at the top of the road emerges. Alert and attentive, one of my brothers rushes towards the lights, eager to confirm its reason.

As he draws closer to the scene, what unfolds before his eyes leaves him stunned. Two vehicles have been involved in a serious accident. My brother realizes that this is the reason for mom's delay as panic sets in. Quickly assessing the situation, my brother searches for any signs of life. The vehicles lie in disarray, exposing the twisted metal frames as a result of the violence of the collision. All while the EMTs are moving as fast as possible to help all who have been involved. Before my brother could gather himself, mom is pulling away in the ambulance. Immediately he brings us the news of mom's accident. While we are unable to go to the hospital, we patiently wait for the phone to ring. Over the next few hours, we find ourselves in anxious anticipation, fervently hoping that the future holds a miracle.

    Time seems to crawl, and those few hours feel like an eternity. Hours later, the doctor delivers the news we have all been fearing. Mom's spine is severely damaged and her vertebrae just above the C7 of her spine have been broken. The gravity of the situation hits us, and our hearts begin to sink. She will need to undergo major surgery to set the bone back in place.

It is a daunting prospect, but we keep our fingers crossed that the surgery will be successful. However, we soon realize that recovery will not end with the surgery. Soon after her surgery, the whole family gathers at the hospital to show our support and love. The doctors then go into more detail, explaining that ongoing therapy will be essential for her complete recovery. It will be a long road ahead, but our entire family is committed to supporting her every step of the way. While bracing for the challenges ahead, we find reassurance in our family bond. Together, we will work through this long and uncertain journey toward moms recovery. Though the waiting may feel unbearable, the family is determined to stay strong. Firmly believing that the future holds promises of a miracle, we will do everything possible to make it a reality.

While I watch her helplessly in agony, there are moments where I can't help but blame myself. My mind is filled with thoughts that maybe this tragic event would've occurred if I had been a better child. Questions circle profusely through my mind. Did I unknowingly do something to cause her accident? I'm left feeling shameful as these thoughts consume my every breath.

My self-imposed guilt is a constant companion and a heavy burden that I constantly have to bear. But as time passes, so does my mom's healing. And in this moment it offers a sense of relief and optimism. Witnessing her pain and struggles has taken a toll on me, both physically and emotionally. However, as the days go by, I witness her remarkable transformation. I watch as she stays strong and endures through this storm. Her resilience and determination begin to yield results, leading to her healing. It is a testament to the power of perseverance and endurance that resides within her. This pivotal moment symbolizes the end of a chapter filled with lessons and pain. As the brace is removed, a newfound sense of freedom permeates the air. It is a turning point that brings about a profound change within the entire family.

 One that will change every one of us forever. Just a week or so after mom has her brace removed, her desire to find God takes center stage. As mom sits me down to talk, she begins explaining to me how she almost died that day on the road. Thus in turn wants to seek change for the whole family. She goes on to say that the day she was on the way back from the store, a voice told her not to put her seat belt on. She then reveals that the doctors told her that if she had, she may not be alive today. She believes that God was the One who spoke to her and desperately wanted us to know who saved her life. I can't quite understand what she is telling me yet but soon I will. All I know is that she is safe and that is all that matters. Even while mom has known God for many years, I remain unaware of who this God is that she now speaks of. Intrigued by her unwavering faith and the positive impact God has on her life, I am compelled to go on a journey of discovery. I yearn to understand what it is about this connection with God that brings her so much peace and strength.

As the days unfold, my mom's newfound devotion draws in the whole family. Together, we explore the realms of spirituality and faith, engaging in heartfelt conversations while seeking answers to our deepest questions. Through this process, I am exposed to different perspectives and teachings, gradually piecing together the puzzle of who this God is that my mom has embraced. While knowing things need to get better for my brothers and me, my mother seeks God and His Word.

And once again, I begin to have questions. Who is this God? Where has He been? Why can't I see Him? Curiosity fills my mind as I ponder these questions. My mother sits us down and begins to tell us all about God. She explains that God is the creator of the universe, who has been with us since the beginning. He is loving, merciful, and always present, even though we may not see Him with our physical eyes. Instead, we can feel His presence through believing and His love through the people around us. Some may think that I should blame God for my past. But surprisingly, I am led to do the complete opposite. If this God is truly who my mom says He is then maybe He can help me.

Even though I am angry, bitter, and hurt, I long for love. But not just any type of love, real authentic love. Maybe this God can give me what I've so longed for. In my heart, I just can't see myself trusting and loving a God who could ever hurt or abandon me. If that is who this God is then I'm better off walking alone. My heart tells me to pursue Him, so that's just what I intend to do. Mother's desire to find a church consists of being part of a community of believers that can help us grow spiritually.

I have so many things to ask Him and I want to know Him. Mom wants us to have a place where we can learn more about God, worship Him, and connect with others who share in the faith. As I listen to my mother's desire to find a church, excitement fills my heart. Maybe this God that she speaks of can indeed answer the deep questions that lurk behind every door in my mind. Perhaps, by embracing all my mother has to offer us, I can open myself up to a new world of understanding. I am eager to explore and learn more about this God who seems so mysterious.

With an open mind and an open heart, I am prepared to see where this path leads me. Just as quickly as the tables turn, so does my faith. At the age of ten, I humbly accept God into my life by confessing Romans 10:9-10. God is now joining on this journey through life. As I become more curious about Him, so does my eagerness to attend church. Until now, I felt alone on this journey and wondered if I would always walk alone. Without God, I was heading to an eternal death. I'm extremely grateful that God saw in me what I couldn't see. I've been chosen to be a part of His family and in due time everything will make sense. Knowing now that I have God by my side brings my soul comfort and reassurance. It's a feeling I can't put into words, but now I'm filled with hope. I'm alive and reborn into God's Kingdom. Attending church is becoming a crucial part of my spiritual journey. It's a place where I can connect with others who share similar beliefs and learn more about God's teachings. Sermons and worship services provide me with guidance and direction, helping me to deepen my understanding. My eagerness to deepen my relationship with God continues. I am excited to discover more about His teachings, His love, and His plan for my life.

With God by my side, I am filled with confidence and courage. As I embrace this new chapter of my life, I am grateful that God is my companion. I am longing to see how my faith continues to evolve and will shape the person I will become. With each step I take, I remember I am not walking alone anymore and I am truly blessed. Getting involved with the ministry has had a profound impact on my ability to cope with my past. While I still find the understanding of God and His ways to be a mystery, I am committed to diligently seeking growth in this area.

In the depths of my being, I am immensely thankful for the efforts my mother has made in my life. Although my current circumstances may not be ideal, the presence of God in my life brings me wholeness and vitality. My eyes have been opened to God's love. Church feels like a second home to me. The knowledge that is imparted in God's Word is truly remarkable. It equips me with the understanding of how to engage in spiritual battles in the right manner. Even though it would be dishonest to claim that all my pain has vanished, the presence of God in my life has made a significant difference.

His guidance and support have become my invaluable resource. Just a simple touch of His love fills me with a newfound sense of peace. A sense in which I have never experienced before. The burdens I face are no longer mine, they belong to God. Even though I cannot physically see Him, I can feel His presence and know that He is with me every step of the way. His love and grace transform my perspective, and I am forever grateful for the valuable lessons. Wanting to be closer to the ministry, we travel an hour into Houston every Sunday and Wednesday for fellowship.

The commitment and dedication mom shows to her faith are truly admirable. However, after a few months, the long drive starts to affect the entire family. The idea of moving closer to the ministry arises. Houston is undeniably a big city with its own set of opportunities and challenges. Being closer to the ministry would mean being more connected to the community. On the other hand, it also means leaving behind familiar surroundings and uprooting our lives. It is perfectly understandable to have mixed feelings about such a significant decision. As time goes on, my own belief and faith start to grow even stronger. I have come to realize that making decisions by faith is extremely important.

It is not merely about the physical proximity to the ministry but also the sense of belonging it brings. Moving to Houston may allow me to immerse myself fully in the teachings of fellowship. Moving might be daunting, but it is important to consider the potential benefits. In turn, it could bring new friendships and connections with like-minded individuals who share a similar faith. Ultimately, the decision to move closer to the ministry is a personal one. It requires careful consideration, weighing the pros and cons, and listening to my own heart. It is a journey of faith and trust, where I must seek guidance from God. Hopefully, I can find the courage to make decisions that align with my heart. But even though my choice is valued by God, it is ultimately moms decision to make this move. As the questions once again resurface, I'm left wanting to know many answers. Is this the best decision? Will I be strong enough to let go? What will happen to all the animals? Will mom be able to find them a good home?

Chapter 3

Taking a leap of faith

In the summer of 1994, after many months of preparation the entire family sets out to move. Filled with anticipation, I receive the news that we are moving to Alief, a community inside Houston. So I make a conscious effort to view the move as a fresh start, in hopes that my past will stay hidden. My family has a lot of work ahead, such as finding a new home, packing our belongings, and making all the necessary arrangements for the animals. It is a hectic time, but my mom is determined to make the transition as smooth as possible. As the days go by, I find myself both excited and nervous about the drastic move. Houston is a big city with unfamiliar surroundings and people. It is an opportunity for me to explore a different environment and make new friends. The thought of leaving behind everything I know and starting over is daunting. As I wonder what will happen to all the animals I find myself full of sadness. The horses have touched me in a new and refreshing way. But letting go, especially the horses, will not be easy. They hold a special place in my heart and have been my source of comfort. Their majestic presence and the bond we share make it difficult to say goodbye. With the horse's strong and graceful bodies, flowing manes, and expressive eyes, their beauty is undeniable. They have been more than just companions; they have been my confidants.

Through them, I have learned patience, empathy, and the power of a gentle touch. It is a bittersweet moment, but now the time has come to part ways. The thought of leaving them weighs heavily on my heart. But I find comfort in knowing that my mom will find them all good homes. As the day of departure approaches, I remember every moment spent with these magnificent animals. As we pass through town, a sense of finality begins to settle within me. It dawns on me that this may be the last time I lay eyes upon this familiar place. The weight of the move becomes all too real as my heart fills with uneasiness. Adjusting to a new home is not going to be an easy task. It demands patience, resilience, and a willingness to embrace the unknown. As I step on this new terrain, I know it will take time to acclimate. The road ahead is marked with unfamiliar faces and uncharted territories. It is a path that requires me to step out of my comfort zone. Doubt may linger in my mind, questioning whether I will ever find my place in this new environment. But to my surprise, from the first moment I step foot into the city, a sense of loneliness sets in.

    The bustling streets are overwhelming. But with the summer passing fast, the time has come for me to begin school. Walking through the school gates for the first time, I can't help but feel a knot in my stomach. Everyone around me is a stranger. Their faces are unknown and their stories are untold. The hallways echo with laughter and conversations, making me feel like an outsider in this new environment. The city is teeming with people, all moving at a much faster pace than I am accustomed to. It feels as if everyone is in a constant rush, racing against time. Yet, amidst the chaos, I take a deep breath and attempt to embrace my surroundings. This is my new reality, and I have no choice but to adapt. I long to fit in here, to find friends who understand and accept me for who I am. But the path to belonging requires the courage to step out into the unknown. I take one step at a time embracing each endeavor that comes my way.

By immersing myself in school activities in the hope that the walls of loneliness will soon crumble. The city may be big, and its people may be strangers, but I am determined to find my place. I will not be discouraged by the fast pace and sea of unfamiliar faces. I take another step with each passing day. But, no matter how much I hide my hurt, things will only grow more intense. Despite my efforts to bury my pain, it resurfaces and haunts my thoughts. I was hoping that by moving to a new city my past would be left behind. But I have been mistaken. No matter how hard I try, it's a relentless force that I can't ignore. For many years now, I've wanted to be with a man. Since I was raped I've struggled to overcome this desire. The desperate need for comfort in the arms of another man becomes overwhelming. It consumes my every waking moment, and the fear of what lies ahead becomes a constant worry. I am torn between the longing for love and the potential consequences that may come. Trying to ignore this sensation only pushes me closer to the arms of another.

The pull gets stronger the more I resist. Fate seems to be guiding me toward an inevitable decision.

Not knowing how to overcome this urge, I can no longer deny its existence. In my quest for a distraction, I stumble upon a handsome man. Our paths cross unexpectedly, and a connection begins to form. We find companionship with one another, sharing stories and experiences that resonate deeply within. With each passing day, our bond becomes stronger. We support each other through the ups and downs, providing a safe space to be vulnerable without judgment. With my curiosity getting the best of me, I find myself yearning for something much deeper. Of course, I love the friendship but my flesh wants more. Being just a friend is becoming a dangerous path to tread, one that could lead to unforeseen consequences. I am unable to resist the allure of what could be and all of my evil desires constantly rise. I find myself teetering on the edge of a decision that could change everything. It's a precarious position, one that fills me with both fear and a strange sense of liberation. But my fear gets the best of me just as I gather the courage to leap.

While so close to a deeper connection, I run and the friend I once had has now become a glimpse of my past. The very next day my mother sits me down to talk.

It is with great shock that she and my father are planning a visit to Jordan in jail. I haven't heard that name in years. A mix of disbelief and confusion wash over me. The questions arise once again. What on earth could they possibly have to discuss with him? And why now? Jordan's therapist has requested a meeting with both my mom and dad. He has something important to share that is crucial to his healing process. My mind races with questions, skeptical yet curious about what could prompt such a meeting. My thoughts drift back to the past, to the tumultuous days of my childhood. Jordan was always troubled, and mentally disturbed in a way that made him unpredictable. He tormented me relentlessly, leaving me with both physical and emotional pain. And yet, despite it all, a small part of me has always held onto hope that he could find his way out of the darkness. Perhaps this meeting or should I say, therapeutic intervention is what he needs. Maybe, just maybe, it's the key to unlocking a better version of himself. In the face of my pain and trauma, I still harbor a desire for Jordan to find redemption.

It's a complicated sentiment, one that many would not understand. But deep down beneath the layers of my hurt, there still lies a small spark of compassion. My parent's decision to meet with him shows a belief in his potential for change, a belief I have struggled to maintain. So, as mom's words echo in my ears, I find myself torn, hopeful that Jordan can find his way back to the light. It's a delicate balance, one that requires me to set aside my pain and focus on the bigger picture. In the end, I can only hope that this meeting with his therapist is a step toward his transformation. Perhaps it will bring me closer to finding peace. After hours of my mind running wild, my parents finally returns home. Upon their arrival, they decide to sit the entire family down. Mom explains the news that they have come to know. A confession, one that brings to light a dark secret I have held within me for years. Up until now, mom and Jordan are the only ones who knew of this deep dark secret. Jordan, a person I once trusted, admits to sexually abusing me. However, amidst his confession, he adds an untrue statement, claiming that I wanted sex. Who could want sex at the age of seven?

He also admits to trying to burn the house down many years ago. The smoke fire that killed Cheshire had been caused by him. The weight of this awful news crushes my spirit, and I find myself torn, yet again. The news of Jordan's confession is a shattering shock to me and my brothers. I have carried the burden of this secret for years, feeling isolated and alone. But now, knowing that he also killed Cheshire shatters my world even more. The weight of the truth he exposed is immense, and it feels like the ground has been ripped from beneath my feet. The betrayal of trust, coupled with the added trauma of Jordan's statement, leaves me feeling more violated. The tears that stream down my face are not only a manifestation of disgust but also a release of my emotional turmoil. It's a moment of profound vulnerability, one that exposes the deep wounds inflicted by Jordan's actions. But I cannot allow Jordan's statement to define me, even in the face of this devastating revelation.

While his words are hurtful and deeply unjust, I understand that dwelling on them will only prolong my suffering. So, I decide to let go of his false accusations.

With the news of Jordan's confession now out in the open, I need to reclaim my life. The weight of this secret has always been heavy on me, even suffocating. But something inside me has changed, something that I can no longer ignore. Now that this secret is out in the open, what's gonna happen? Will mom press charges on him or will it just fade away into the night? As days pass, nothing is done, and my anger starts to spiral out of control. The confession causes me to rebel with more fury and anger. By admitting this secret, I have unleashed a beast within me that refuses to be tamed. As a result, I begin running the streets. Being rebellious against mom seems to be the only way for me. I just can't understand why she wouldn't give me the necessary justice my heart severely deserves. I'm a complete mess because of Jordan and I hate that I'm so angry. I feel so helpless. But I know I must be strong so I cry out to God! In hopes that He can ease my symptoms, I embrace Him. With each step, I feel the shackles of expectations breaking away, leaving behind a trail of defiance. No longer will I be confined by the judgments and opinions of others.

It is time for me to forge my path, regardless of the consequences. I'm filled with such heavy disappointment and hurt but rebellion comes with a price. At the age of twelve, I turn to cigarettes. As I take my first puff, I'm filled with an overwhelming calmness. It's at that very moment I find myself addicted. The need for nicotine will only add to the mess. The constant smoke inhalation grows more and more every day. Every chance I get, I steal one or two here and there from mom's pack. Not thinking ahead anymore, I rest in the thought of the temporary fix cigarettes give me. Once again, my longing for a man comes to the surface. It's not just a desire for companionship, but a yearning to be seen and understood. I crave the touch of another human being. I rebel as if my defiance is desperate to fill the void from within. After my close encounter with a companion some time ago, my desire for a man's touch greatly intensifies. In July of 1995, at the age of twelve, I venture into the unknown, throwing no caution into the wind. As I dive deeper into this reckless pursuit, I am tangled in a web of dangerous liaisons and risky encounters. The dangerous nature of my rebellion fuels my desire for more, pushing me further into the darkness.

As I stumble into the dark, I find myself attracted to someone. We begin to hang out, and things quickly shift into gear. After that first evening, our relationship becomes serious. We spend more time together, getting to know each other better and forming a bond. However, our happiness is short-lived when my mom discovers our relationship and vehemently forbids us from seeing each other. It is heart-wrenching, as we are both deeply in love and couldn't bear being separated. The questions that continue to surface, once again need answers. Am I truly in love? Is that even possible at the age of twelve? Determined to be together, one evening we hatch a plan. I decide to sneak out of my window, hoping for us to run away together. As I carefully climb out of my second-floor window he stands down below with open arms. He ensures my safe descent to the ground. I take a deep breath, gathering all the courage I can muster and jump. But as fate would have it, he doesn't catch me in time and I slip through his hands. The impact to the ground is sudden and harsh, leaving me in agony. Pain surges through my body, leaving me momentarily paralyzed.

Tears begin to form as the impact of the fall is overwhelming. The reality of our forbidden love and the consequences of our actions hit immediately. I realize the depth of his love for me as we sit there, surrounded by darkness and uncertainty. Our love is strong, and we are determined to fight for it, no matter the cost. In that vulnerable moment, with the taste of rebellion and the sting of pain still fresh, we make a silent vow to each other. We promise to navigate through the obstacles ahead, holding onto each other tightly, and never letting go. But when mom discovers I'm sneaking out, she decides to take more serious measures. She places bolts and locks on the doors and windows. Doing this causes me and my companion to grow distant. As I act in rage, I find myself breaking the windows. When she padlocks the doors, I take the key from under her pillow, vanishing into the night. The taste of freedom is fresh on my lips. With my disobedience drawing stronger mom is desperate for help. She wonders if moving me away will be the next best option. She begins to wonder if this method of coping is beneficial for my well-being.

The situation has escalated to the point where I cannot communicate effectively. My bitterness has reached an unhealthy level. So, one night around 2 am, I impulsively kicked out the window and make my way to a friend's house. I hope my absence will go unnoticed and in turn, allow me some time away. But the next morning, mom is there to greet me. In the face of ongoing struggles with running away and battling depression, the decision has been made for me to be admitted to the Harris County Psychiatric Ward. My mother hopes this step will lead to finding a solution to my problems. Despite my doubts, it is important to acknowledge that moms decision is rooted in a genuine desire to help. She believes that the Harris County Psychiatric Ward will provide the necessary support to help me overcome my struggles. While I may be skeptical, I understand her concern and the love that drives her actions. It is important to consider the potential benefits of the Harris County Psychiatric Ward. This facility is equipped with trained professionals who specialize in psychiatric care. They have the knowledge and experience to address various mental health issues, including depression. By admitting me to this facility, I'm provided with a structured environment to receive support.

The Harris County Psychiatric Ward offers various therapeutic interventions, such as individual and group therapy, which may help me address the underlying causes of my problems. They have access to medications that play a role in managing my depression. Even though no one has tried to help in the past, this may be just what I need. The professionals here are committed to helping me with my mental health challenges and finding effective solutions. While it is natural to question whether this time will be different, it is crucial to give them a chance. I try to keep my sanity intact because right now, I'm afraid and feeling hopeless The world around me feels overwhelming. Once I arrive at the medical facility, the doctors and therapists welcome me with warm smiles and reassuring words. Their presence alone provides a moment of peace in the darkness. Tears fall profusely down my cheeks as I wait to be evaluated by a counselor. Each drop carries fear, sadness, and vulnerability. It's as if the world's weight has become too heavy for me to bear. With God in the distance, the static in my head intensifies. A sense of anticipation and apprehension fills me as I'm called into the holding area.

    The counselors ask me questions, delving deep into the core of my emotions. How I answer these questions will shape the path toward finding a suitable treatment for my depression. It is a critical moment that may hold the key to my recovery. My depression, like a dark cloud hanging over me every moment, desperately needs intervention. The counselors carefully assess my condition and consider various treatment options. After a thorough evaluation, they decide that I could benefit from medication. Zoloft is prescribed, a medication known to provide relief from the grip of depression. It is not a magic cure but a tool to help me regain control over my emotions and stabilize my life. But with the need for emotional stitches, I need a more permanent way to heal.

I have been carrying these burdens for far too long. In the depths of emotional wounds, I often yearn for a remedy that will give me some lasting relief. If only I could realize that leaning on God has the power to change the outcome, perhaps things may be different. Yet, my emotions blind me, preventing me from feeling His presence. In my misguided state, I have chosen to separate myself from Him, thus embracing disobedience.

During my time in the psychiatric ward, I reflect upon the urge to run away again. Even though I face so much adversity, I still choose to be disobedient. However, this time, I am determined to approach the situation differently. Being doped up on Zoloft will not fix the problems that lurk in the shadows. My mind begins to run even more rampant as I plot another escape from reality. Running from my problems becomes an addiction like no other. I believe I can ensure a different outcome by making smarter decisions and preparing adequately. No matter how much my mom tries to keep me from trouble, it never works. Living within this psychiatric ward's walls for six months is dreadful, and I can't wait to be released. Right now, I am only touching the surface of the true reality hidden deep behind my eyes. I am trapped in a nightmare, and my only desire is to be free. Within the confines of these walls, I have been stripped of my freedom. Every day feels like a battle as I cope with the psychiatric treatments and therapies. The doctors and nurses mean well, but their efforts can only do so much. The medication they prescribe numbs my mind, making me feel detached from the world around me.

Despite my resistance to their help, I know deep down that I am only hurting myself. But it's hard to see beyond the suffocating darkness that is engulfing my thoughts and emotions. This nightmare that I am trapped in feels never-ending. The pain I carry within me is indescribable, continually weighing me down. It's as if I am drowning in a sea of despair, in need of air. But finally, six months later, after enduring what feels like an eternity, I'm released I can finally taste the sweet freedom. But this time, something is different. I have found my escape again, and I'm determined more than ever before. As I step outside, the sunlight hits my face, warming my weary soul. The drugs that the Psych Ward placed in me have only temporarily numbed my pain. I hated the way they made me feel so I vowed to never take another pill for depression. The uneasy feeling it gave makes me extremely uncomfortable. Now, off the meds and out of the Psych Ward my issues resurface. Every morning as I wake up, I'm greeted with depression and anxiety. Not long after returning home, the thought of running hits me like a two-ton truck!

Running away seems like the only option to ease my painful memories. Lost, I'm just running like a hamster on a wheel. I am left with no choice but to trust in the unknown. As I take the first step toward my uncertain future, I can't help but feel the adrenaline coursing through my veins. While I head out into the world, I sense immediate tension being released. The weight of the past slowly lifts off my shoulders but it doesn't go very far. During a tumultuous experience, where memories threaten to be suffocated, a perfect plan emerges. But my perfect plan has not been carefully charted as the relentless hunger for shelter grows. The insatiable need for food and shelter becomes a barrier, isolating me from everyone and everything. The despair of an unending nightmare propels me further into the dark. The tension in the air thickens as my need for shelter turns into fear. With every step I take, I am determined to put as much distance between myself and the past. I spend that whole night trying to figure out what to do next. Thoughts swirl in my head like a storm, each one vying for attention. With nowhere safe to go, confusion and uneasiness start to rise.

Should I seek help, or should I continue to hide in the shadows? Fear grips me tightly as I weigh the options, knowing that any decision I make could have dire consequences. The darkness of the night matches the turmoil within me as I grapple with the uncertainty of my future. The frailty of life is now a stark reality, and I am haunted by the choices I have made. Each noise I hear, each shadow I see, sends a shiver down my spine. Being all alone on the streets is terrifying but I ignore every warning sign. The specter of death looms large, a constant reminder of the fragility of my existence. There is an endless loop of fear and adrenaline etched into my memory. Each passing moment intensifies my uneasiness from within. This constant companion whispers doubts and fears into my ear. I feel as if I am teetering on the edge of a cliff, unsure of which way to turn. Walking to nowhere, I run into a figure standing in the shadows. The encounter is unexpected, and I freeze in place. Is this possibly who I may need right now? My heart rate increases as I prepare myself for what's to come.

But to my shock, the shadow lurking in the distance is a police officer. He walks up to me and asks for my identification. Hoping he won't find out that I'm a runaway, I nervously explain to him that I don't have any. The officer then asks me how old I am, and his stern gaze makes me even more anxious. With a trembling voice, I tell him that I'm thirteen years old. After asking my name, he proceeds to his vehicle and tells me to stay put. After running my name, he places me under arrest. My heart sinks as I realize he intends to take me to juvenile. As the officer places me into the car, fear overtakes me, and my mind races with thoughts of escaping. My mind goes into overdrive as I dread what is to come. My heart sinks even further as the car comes to a stop. As I see the imposing building that will become my temporary home, I start to regret my actions. The officer escorts me inside, and I can't help but feel a sense of fear. The unfamiliar surroundings and the presence of other troubled youths only intensify my anxiety.

As I'm led to my cell, I can't help but wonder how my life has come to this. Thoughts of my family, particularly my mom, flood my mind. The sense of isolation and despair grows stronger with each passing moment. In the cold and dreary cell, I find myself contemplating the events that led me here. Questions within my head lead me to wonder when and if I will ever see the light again. Until then, I have found the strength to sustain myself through this unfamiliar territory. I yearn for another chance, an opportunity to rebuild my life and make amends for my past mistakes. After twenty-four long hours, I'm informed that I am being released into my mom's care. The authorities make it clear that if I continue to disobey, I could face the consequences of returning. But even as dreadful as being at home may be, I can't help but miss the streets. Despite the warnings, I can't shake off the feeling of freedom. My constant actions of running away have become an addiction. But, once again in an attempt to flee, a few days later, the cops find me. Here I am, back in jail. If I thought overnight was rough, this time will be longer. But before being released this time, I must go before the judge. I thought I would just get another slap on my wrist, but this time the consequences are more severe.

The thrill of the chase and the adrenaline have been pumping through my veins. But now the consequences are catching up to me, and it's time to face the music. The judge's stern gaze pierces through me as I stand before her. By the look on her face, I can see that she is not pleased with my repeated running away offense. The judge's voice echoes in the courtroom as she announces my sentence. This time I'm demanded to spend one week in the West Dallas juvenile detention center. A week may not seem like a long time, but it's an eternity in a detention center. As I prepare for the weeks ahead, all I can do is feel helpless. I have no choice but to wait it out. Escaping the detention center is impossible. So now I must sit here and contemplate a better move when I'm released. Even though I hate being in juvie, I hate being at home even more.

In my mind, running away is better than being at home. Due to many years of anger and hurt, my pain has turned into a sense of heartless action. All of the jail sentences will not fix my problems. Before being released for the second time, the judge places me on a year's probation. This new finding comes with rules and expectations and she hopes that this will stop me from running away. Now with my back up against the wall, I have no choice but to accept the judge's terms. But the minute I make it home, the urge to run grows even stronger. Not even a month into my release, I violate probation and it leads me back to jail. Being behind these walls is not where I've envisioned myself and I don't know how to stop running away. I'm just so hurt and angry! This vicious cycle continues, escalating into something much more serious. And in 1996, at the age of thirteen, I face the judge again. Throughout the history of my running away, this will be my fifth time being incarcerated, including the Psych Ward. It feels as though no matter what I do, nothing will make a difference. The weight of this hopelessness hangs heavy over me as I brace myself to hear the judge's verdict.

    The judge declares that I must spend six months in the Youth Village, located in Seabrook, TX. My mom is familiar with this place and has requested that I be sent there. I can see the desperation in her eyes as she reaches her breaking point. The Youth Village is often the last resort for teens like me, a final warning before facing the harsh realities of TDC or prison. It is a place where troubled youth are given a chance to change their ways, to find a path toward obedience. My mom and the judge see this as an opportunity for me to receive the help and guidance I desperately need. The Youth Village offers a structured environment to help me confront my issues, learn from my mistakes, and hopefully pave the way for a brighter future. With this sentence, I now find myself at a crossroads. It is a chance to break free from the cycle of self-destructive behavior and embrace the possibility of transformation. Up until now, nothing has seemed to work. Though I may be weary and disheartened, I recognize the importance of this opportunity. After court, while waiting to be transferred to the Youth Village, I can't help but reflect on my past. Everything leading up to this moment has not prepared me for what is about to unfold. The anxiety from within my heart increases. I don't know what to expect from this place.

The anger I feel inside is relenting and I sink deeper into depression. Once it's time to be transported, the weight of the shackles on my hands and feet holds me down. As I walk outside to the transport van, a sense of sadness closes in on me. I'm shackled like I've just robbed or murdered someone. I am a troubled teen but this is too much. All of my disobedience stems from my childhood. As the heavy doors of the Youth Village close behind me, I take a deep breath. I'm ready to face this chapter. Not realizing this place will be a blessing in disguise, I embrace what's to come. In the Youth Village, I will have the support of counselors, mentors, and fellow residents who are all on a similar journey. I strive to learn from my mistakes and cultivate a sense of responsibility. Though the weight of my past may still burden me, I am hopeful that I can shed the shackles of my past. With the support of my mom, and the dedicated staff at the Youth Village, I believe that change is possible. So, as I take my first steps into this new environment, I choose to leave behind the hopelessness that has plagued me up until now. I make my peace in knowing that this place will be my home for the next six months.

Finding myself again is a crucial step in this process because this could be my last chance to make things right. Running away from my past mistakes is no longer the answer. It may have provided temporary relief, but it only prolongs my healing. Instead, I'm learning to confront my past, acknowledge my mistakes, and take responsibility for my actions. My irresponsibility affects both me and everyone around me, including my family. My actions cause damage to the relationships I have with my brothers. The trust that once existed has been shattered, and it will take time and effort to rebuild. My actions over the years have caused them tremendous pain. They try so hard to show me they love me but I'm so broken. I can't see love even if it's right in front of me. I'm desperate for change. I'm tired and I truly need help. I hold onto the hope that one day, through the grace of God, my brothers will find it in their hearts to forgive me. Only God has the power to mend what is broken and heal the wounds that have been inflicted. Breaking free from the vicious cycle of negative behavior and its consequences is difficult. By taking responsibility for my actions, and seeking forgiveness, I can begin to rebuild the relationships that have been damaged. It won't be an overnight process, but with time I believe it may be possible for restoration.

    This boot camp has a unique quality that compels me to dismantle my barriers. But as the walls surrounding my depression were beginning to crumble, I'm confronted with an overwhelming burden. After enduring five months of incarceration, the judge reaches a verdict to extend my sentence by an additional two months. This unexpected decision prolongs my time behind bars. As I hear this news, I'm lost for words. I'm not sure if I will be able to bear this conviction. Why the change in my sentence? Thoughts of suicide begin to form within my mind. Knowing that suicide will destroy my mom I make to choice to press on with my last amount of strength. In doing so I'm able to overcome the thoughts of being caged. By renewing my mind, I come to understand that I must face this head-on. The feeling of being trapped can be overwhelming, but I remind myself that I have the power to break free from any limitations.

    The next few months pass pretty quickly and the time comes for my release. The night before I'm discharged, I decide to make a change for the rest of my life. The experiences I have had during my time here have opened my eyes to the need for change. I recognize the importance of taking responsibility for my actions. From this moment forward, I am committed to making positive choices that will shape my future into something brighter than my past. Being here has taught me to appreciate and respect my mom. In the past, I was so angry about my childhood that I couldn't see beyond my hurt. She has been a constant source of love and support through all of my ups and downs. I realize the sacrifices she has made for me and the unconditional love she has shown. No matter what mistakes I have made in the past, I am grateful for her unwavering presence. Even though we still have unfinished business, I am determined for us to mend our broken ties and adopt a more positive relationship. I now fully understand the importance of forgiveness. Moving on, I am committed to ensuring that it is built on a foundation of understanding and love. Also, I come to know that my relationship with God is important. For many years He has been at the bottom of my list. I've neglected Him and the ministry by placing other things in my life above Him.

However, I know that if I truly want to succeed, God must be my priority. I can lead a more fulfilling life by focusing on more positive and productive endeavors. One of the valuable lessons I have learned from Youth Village is that I'm unable to handle circumstances beyond my control. Life is full of unpredictable situations, and it can be challenging to navigate through things at times. The guidance and support I received from Youth Village equip me with the necessary skills to face anything that comes my way. Starting over can be daunting, but I am blessed to have been given another chance. It is a reminder that no matter how difficult things may seem, there is always a chance for a fresh start. Freedom has never felt so beautiful. For most of my teenage years, I've been trapped mentally, physically, and emotionally. From the age of seven, I've been stripped of my right to be a child. Now here I am at the age of fourteen, having faced incarceration many times. I pray my life can be meaningful, and so I attempt to pursue a future full of faith. Here I go again, questioning the littlest details on this road to freedom! How much longer will I have to fight?

When will the journey in life be content? When will I encounter the spiritual freedom that I so desperately need?

Melissa's Journey " Standing in Freedom " 94

Chapter 4

A newfound love

In the spring of 1998, I chose to leave behind the life I once craved and start a new beginning. As I leave behind everything in my past, I embrace positive things to come. Now ready to start school, I am feeling determined. The uncertainty of starting over is daunting, but I remain hopeful that this change will bring new opportunities. I will try to understand the importance of adapting to my new environment and embracing new experiences. I remind myself that change is a natural part of life, and it is through these changes that I can learn and grow even more. But even while I want to do right, I find myself caught between doing right and wrong. With the internal struggle affecting my motivation to attend school, my desires begin to change. The running away has finally stopped, but another situation arises. Despite only two years having passed since my release from Youth Village, contemplating the idea of quitting school has become my next challenge to endeavor. Deep down, I know that staying in school is the wisest decision, but sadly, I lack any enthusiasm. I so desperately want to do well for myself but my lack of zeal is affecting me strongly.

The battle in my mind is a constant reminder of my failures, chipping away at my motivation and crippling my education journey. Success lies in academic achievements and the ability to reach my goals. Though zeal may elude me, my determination to avoid future regrets is unwavering. I understand that the path to success is paved with challenges. It's vital to find a solution to my overwhelming circumstances, but how? In an attempt to save what strength I have, I ask mom if being homeschooled is a much better solution? I pour out my heart to her, expressing the inner struggles that I've been facing. It is a vulnerable moment as I share my deepest emotions, hoping she will understand and give me support. The weight of not wanting to be a failure hangs heavy on my shoulders. I believe that presenting this idea might be the solution. As I explain the heartfelt desires I have, mom listens attentively. I can see the wheels turning in her mind as she carefully considers my plea.

She promises to think about it, and now the waiting game begins. Itching passing day is filled with anticipation. Finally, just a few weeks later, mom approached me with her decision.

Mom agrees to homeschool me. It feels like a heavy weight has been lifted off my chest. I now have the opportunity to pursue my education in a way that aligns with my needs and aspirations. But I don't fully comprehend the discipline and commitment required in homeschooling to succeed. Not long after I begin homeschooling it becomes evident that this path is not a breeze, but a demanding endeavor. I must learn to manage my time effectively all while staying motivated. The absence of a traditional classroom setting means that I am solely responsible for my progress. It is a daunting task that I am determined to conquer. This moment in life offers a unique opportunity for personal growth. With guidance and support, I can tailor my education to suit my strengths and weaknesses. This flexibility allows me to delve deeper into subjects I am passionate about and explore new areas of interest. One thing that has always been my weakness is that I get bored very easily.

    Distractions are often a problem and as time goes I begin to fall behind on schoolwork. The days become relentless, and my flame to succeed slowly burns out. I find myself failing in each subject. At the age of fifteen, I find myself in another difficult situation. I notice that whenever I come up with a better plan, something always goes wrong. But I'm so caught up in my head that I can't see that. Dropping out of school has never been a part of my plan but my grades are at their ultimate end. If I don't get this right, I may regret it for the rest of my life. So, as I sit here, I seriously weigh my options. I find myself intrigues and mapping out another plan. One that doesn't require me to be in school and my choice becomes evident. So I approach mom and tell her I'd decided to quit and want to get my GED. Mom is not happy with this decision but she supports my reasons. The very next day, mom decides to withdraw me from school. This constant pattern of disappointment leaves me uncertain about where my future may lead because every time I try to forge my path things always seem to fail.

There was a time when I genuinely enjoyed school but that has completely disappeared. The circumstances have somehow transformed me into someone filled with pure laziness. Even while I'm in this state of solitude, I yearn for human connection.

I've been dodging and overlooking this extremely vulnerable craving. The desire to be with someone, to have companionship, becomes increasingly pronounced. It is in these moments that I remember the importance of meaningful relationships. Reflecting on my circumstances, my journey takes another unexpected turn. In a quiet neighborhood down the street, a man captures my attention, and over time, we find ourselves spending more and more time together. As our connection deepens, feelings blossom between us, leading us down an unpredictable path. Little do I know that a life-altering event would soon test our fate. Caught in the moment and disregarding the potential repercussions, we engage in a physical relationship. Despite taking precautions and ensuring our safety through protection, fate has a different plan in store. I discover I am pregnant, an unexpected twist that would confuse an already complicated life. The news of my pregnancy hit me like a ton of bricks. Until that moment, the thought of becoming a mother has never crossed my mind, and now, it looms heavy and daunting.

Melissa's Journey " Standing in Freedom "

The consequences of my choices loom ominously. My life, already filled with its fair share of challenges, suddenly feels even more uncertain. I'm afraid to talk with mom about this inevitable conversation. She is still quite upset about me quitting school. Nervous and quite fearful, I find myself grappling with the weight of this newfound responsibility. As I stand at the crossroads on this journey, I'm overwhelmed with a whirlwind of emotions. Fear, confusion, and a sense of isolation become constant companions. The future that once seemed within reach is now shrouded in disappointment. Questions once again plague my mind. How will I cope with this unexpected development? How will it impact my dreams, aspirations, and the life I have meticulously wanted for myself? How will I take care of a child at fifteen? How many more mistakes will I make before I learn? Even though I'm feeling overwhelmed, I must gather my strength. Despite the uncertainty of the situation, I embrace this uncharted territory. With no job and no money, I can't see a way. This time my choice is bringing another life into an already messed up situation. Seeking after love in all the wrong places leads me to this place. The whole time God has been waiting for me to come home, but what do I do? Run! Something I said I would never do again but yet here I am.

My heart yearns for God, but my mind blocks Him out. With a heavy heart, I put one foot in front of the other and keep walking. This is my mess to untangle, a web of decisions that I must figure out on my own. It's scary and overwhelming, but I know deep down that I can find the strength from within to make it through this storm. Knowing that I can't keep this a secret, I gather the courage to tell the father that I'm pregnant. Something within me is hoping for his support. But instead, he denies the child and rejects the very existence of our unborn baby. The weight of his rejection crashes down on me, entangling me in a sea of sadness and despair. How could I have been with someone who would treat me this way? This question lingers in my mind, echoing through the empty spaces of my heart. It's a painful realization, a bitter pill to swallow. But amidst the heartache, from within I find a glimmer of strength growing. I refuse to let this define me, to let myself be consumed by the actions of another.

Fear and anxiety fill my heart as I dread telling mom. In order for me to get the guidance and support I need, I must confide in her.

Despite the anxiety that grips me, I understand the importance of sharing this burden with her. So I am ready to face whatever comes my way. I take a deep breath and prepare myself for our conversation. I prepare as best as I can, with thoughts of having an abortion echoes in my mind. As mom and I speak she explains that while she is disappointed with the circumstances, she supports my decision to have an abortion. So I set an appointment and await the day. The very next week as nervousness draws near I head to the clinic. Doubt and fear start setting in, bringing even more confusion. For a second I almost backed out of this decision as I question my choices. Who could've prepared my heart for this one? How could I know what this would do to me? As a woman, I'm freely given a choice, but the pain I have to endure comes with a cost. While I proceed with this harsh decision, my emotions are placed to the side. Upon leaving the clinic, a wave of sadness rushes through my soul. Something in this very instant has completely changed. I no longer feel like the same person.

Already broken, this leaves me with an overwhelming sense of regret. I find it hard to make sense of my thoughts even amid theses swirling emotions. The decision weighs heavily on my conscience, and I question if it was the right choice. But even if it is, I can't erase what has happened. Realizing I can't go back and change the past, I seek solace in the comfort of silence. The shame and blame that I place on myself is relentless. The conflicting feelings of relief and sorrow mingle, creating a complex tapestry of emotions that I struggle to untangle. As I steer through the aftermath, I can't help but wonder about the impact this choice will have on my future. As my sadness rises so do my questions. How will I be able to move forward without carrying the burden of this regret? Will the pain I have endured be worth it in the end? Will God still love me? These questions haunt me as the answers elude my grasp. The sterile walls and the scent of antiseptic linger in my memory. These memories are constantly reminding me of the difficult decision I made that day. The weight of my emotions feels unbearable. It's as if the heaviness of my heart could pull me down into an abyss of frantic despair.

Trying to block out that dreadful memory, I retreat into the quiet corners of my world where I can find rest from the internal chaos. In these moments of silence, I allow myself to grieve. I wholeheartedly process the emotions that threaten to overwhelm me. I find the strength to face another day even in this state. In time, I hope to find healing, peace, and forgiveness. Even with so many regrets, one day I hope to regain my self-worth. Before I have the chance to overcome losing a child, I'm met face to face with the opportunity of a lifetime. This choice will bring so many things my way. My once-broken life begins to take the next course of direction. One evening, a few months after my abortion, while riding my bike, I'm stopped by a handsome man. He introduces himself as Rick. But instead of asking for my number, he asks for my address. This gesture tickles me, and I give it to him. A few days later, he knocks on my door. I politely invite him in and we sit for hours getting to know one another. From there, our connection grows stronger. He is charming and has a great sense of humor.

Our conversations are filled with laughter and genuine interest in each other's lives. We share stories about our past and our dreams for the future. Even though we have just met it is as if we have known each other for years. As time goes on, we discover more and more similarities between one another. Our compatibility seems almost too good to be true. Everything is going so well and things start moving faster in our relationship. Several months later, the subject of having a child arises. Even though I'm now only sixteen, I feel my heart is pointing me in the right direction. Rick is a wonderful man, and I can already see that he will be an outstanding father. With this in mind, we contemplate having a child. Although my mom likes him, she is unaware we are discussing a family. The choice to have a child at such a young age is significant. However, we believe that with love, support, and determination, we can provide our child with a loving and nurturing environment. As time goes on, we come to find out that we are pregnant. Being pregnant with Rick's child seems so right, but telling mom makes me nervous.

    Knowing that I have to tell her the news, I wait for the right moment. So, one day when I have her alone, I drop the news on mom. Immediately she gets upset and becomes furious with me.

Deep down, I know that she doesn't want me to be hurt again. But with no other choice but to accept our decision, she comes around and accepts my pregnancy. As the weeks pass, I am left with the excitement of seeing this baby growing in my belly. From the first moment I see my child on the ultrasound, I become overwhelmed with excitement. Seeing the tiny heartbeat flickering on the screen fills me with joy and anticipation. Every ultrasound appointment allows me to witness my child's growth and development. It is a fascinating experience to watch my baby's features become more defined. Feeling my child kick inside my womb is another magical aspect of this pregnancy. The gentle flutters gradually transform into more vigorous movements. It is a constant reminder of the miracles happening inside my body. Just when I think things couldn't improve, we receive the news that we are having a boy. The excitement multiplies as we imagine all the adventures and experiences we would share.

    We name him Rick Junior. With the joy of expecting a baby boy, we have many plans for our birthing methods. After careful consideration, I decide to try a midwife-assisted birth. I am drawn to a supportive and personalized approach to childbirth. With me being born at home, I want to walk in my mom's footsteps and do the same with Junior. Hoping for a memorable birth experience, I eagerly embrace my decision. The midwife's expertise and personalized care will ensure that my baby and I receive the support we need throughout the process. As I continue on this pregnancy journey, I am grateful for the opportunity to bring new life into the world. I eagerly await the arrival of my little Rick Junior, cherishing each moment of this incredible chapter. And on April 11, 1999, labor begins so we grab our bags and head to the midwife. As the labor pains intensify I'm struggling to control the contractions and regulate my breathing. Despite initially planning for a home birth, the circumstances quickly change. The plan is not going as smoothly as anticipated. This pain is unbearable, and I need help. No one could have prepared me for the intensity of these contractions. They are unexplainably painful.

Understanding the urgency and need for medical intervention, my midwife swiftly transfers me to the hospital. I have always envisioned a calm and serene environment. One that is surrounded by loved ones. But sometimes, the unknown can challenge us in ways we could never imagine. So, as I head to the hospital, I hope that medical professionals can alleviate the pain. Upon arriving, the medical team swiftly takes charge. The pain slowly subsides with an epidural, allowing me to focus on the anticipation of meeting my baby. I feel safe knowing that I have a team of medical professionals by my side, guiding me through the process. After hours of contractions and pushing, the time is finally here! On the evening of April 11, 1999, makes his way into this world. He is such a precious baby, and I can't help but cry tears of joy. All I wanna do is stay here right where I'm at and never let him go. After a few days of remaining at the hospital, the time comes when we can return home. The feeling of anxiousness overtakes me as we drive away from the hospital. I can't wait to enjoy my days watching him grow.

    As I lay down after such an exhausting few days, I doze off and dream wonderful dreams. I feel peace rekindling within my soul. Having Junior brings me such contentment. The connection we have fills my heart with warmth and tranquility.

The love and joy I feel for him is overwhelming. His presence in my life brings me newfound happiness. In his embrace, I find comfort, and in his smile, I find everlasting peace. Two months pass like lightning and the bond we share is unwavering. My heart melts every time I stare into his eyes. Seeing him so peacefully in my arms, I am taken back by my newfound love. Not wanting this moment to end, I hold him close to my heart. I hold onto the plans I have for his future while capturing every beautiful moment with him. Everything seems to be so perfect. I have the love of my life and my son. But on June 21, 1999, the clouds hung low as the rain fills the sky. As I ignore the essence all around me, I feel blessed to have yet another day with my family. As I get into the rhythm of my day, the time comes to feed Junior his mid-day meal. After feeding him, I lay Junior down so he can take a nap.

Upon resting for a few hours, Rick, his dad, goes to wake him up. Once Rick attempts to wake him, he finds him not breathing. Time stops and the world around me falls to the floor. Full of panic, it feels as if our world has frozen. Immediately we rush to the hospital. The medical team tries for a long time to revive Junior. As I sit there I long for this horrible nightmare to end but it doesn't. There are not enough words to describe the amount of pain that courses through my body. No matter what the doctors try, reviving Junior is no longer viable. On the evening of June 21, 1999, we are given the news that he has passed. This devastating event shatters my heart and my whole world turns upside down. The pain and grief I feel as if I've been thrown into a blender and shredded to pieces. In the midst of my anguish, I find myself questioning things. How could this be happening? Why has he left me? Just hours ago, I was holding Junior in my arms and the next, he is gone. The weight of guilt on my heart causes bitterness to consume my soul.

Endless pain plagues my mind, pulling me further away from reality. I've drifted into a sea of sadness. Every day becomes a struggle as I try to make sense of this tragedy. After the coroner performs the autopsy we come to find that our son has passed from SIDS. Not quite understanding I find out that SIDS is short for Sudden Infant Death Syndrome. It's hard right now for me to wrap my mind around this whole situation so as I grieve the loss of my son, I pray to God for comfort. Having to prepare for his funeral becomes an even higher hill to climb. It's really hard to think about this when I never saw this happening in the first place. With little strength going through my veins, we call upon the family to help. They can raise the money needed to bury him and to have a small service. This is the hardest trial that I've ever had to face. God's strength is the only thing keeping me alive right now. I portray myself to have it together but inside I'm dying. Within my soul, everything feels like a dream that I'm desperate to wake up from. The numbness and lack of mental clarity leads me into emotional isolation.

As we lay him to rest, a deep sense of heartbreak overtakes my heart. I'm determined to press on only because of God's strength. I will always cherish the memories we had together and hold onto the bond we shared. Junior may have passed away, but his memory will forever live on in my heart. Though the pain may linger, I strive to find acceptance in the face of this awful tragedy. Losing my son has done something to me and I will never be the same. Thus making it hard for me to get a grip on my sanity.

Over and over again, I tell myself that this can't be real. The weight of my sorrow grows heavier with each passing moment. The truth of reality hasn't fully set in yet and my zombie-like presence makes me hesitant. Every breath I take reminds me of the void of my firstborn. All I want to do right now is to wake up. So desperately I want this to be a figment of my imagination. Yet, as the days go on, his absence remains unyielding. My depression becomes another set of silent challenges for me to overcome. The ache in my soul intensifies, and my mind begins to wander. I find myself lost in a storm of emotions, drifting further away from the shores of stability.

  The grip of sorrow tightens its hold on my fragile heart. The waves of sadness crash against the soft vessel of my being, threatening to consume me entirely. In this emotional state, my thoughts become tangled, and clarity becomes a distant fantasy. But my resilience remains even within the darkness. I refuse to let despair completely consume me in an attempt to return to the shores. I will not allow myself to be consumed even though the road may be treacherous with pain that's insurmountable.

I won't let grief define me even when my heart aches, and my breath is entangled with sadness. Within my soul lies a resilience that refuses to be extinguished. I trust that the sun will rise again one day and cast its gentle warmth upon my weary heart. Rick and my family have been invaluable during this challenging time. Their love and understanding have given me the strength and courage to face each day. I honestly don't know how I would have kept moving without their unwavering support. As I progress in my journey I find the strength to press on. And a few months after Junior's passing, I receive unexpected news that I'm pregnant. This time, I am emotionally unprepared to welcome another child into the world.

The grief and pain from losing Junior is still daunting, and I need more time. Rick and I find ourselves facing a difficult decision. With the loss of Junior still lingering, I don't know if I have the energy to make the right choice. After discussing our options, we make the painful choice to have an abortion. It's a decision we do not take lightly but one that we believe is necessary. We lean on each other for support during this time, relying on the love that has brought us together. Despite everything I've learned, I still struggle with forgiving myself. As the lack of forgiveness resonates within my mind I begin to question myself. God has already forgiven me, so why can't I forgive myself? Why do I make things harder on myself? My prayer is to one day forgive myself and let go of all my bitterness. So much has happened throughout my life. I'm only seventeen now and I've made so many terrible mistakes. Placing my attention on more positive situations will help to distance myself from the pain. I've come to know that with time, even the most devastating wounds can be healed. In September 2000 Rick and I became pregnant again.

    With all of my past mistakes, I can't believe we are here again but I refuse to have another abortion. After taking a moment to think, we decide to keep this child. In the past few years, I have lost too many children and it's not fair to do this again. The Lord has given me a second chance, and I am extremely grateful. I have to face this decision head-on this time. Only a few months into the pregnancy, we receive news that I'm pregnant with another boy.

With this child being a miracle baby we decide to name him Juvon. This wonderful news overwhelms me with joy. With Junior, I didn't get the chance to share many memories. So I set my heart on sharing many memories with Juvon. With every ultrasound picture I see, a little more of my heart is captured. Excited about the future I begin to prepare for delivery. After tons of research, I choose Bellaire Hospital in Houston, TX. It's a small and inviting hospital where I come to find comfort. I am confident that here I will receive the best birthing plan. As I watch Juvon develop in the womb, I long to hold him in my arms.

The anticipation gets stronger with each passing moment. Time flies and the preparation for his welcome is around the corner. On the morning of Friday, June 15, 2001, upon waking I feel a sharp pain in my stomach. I remember what contractions feel like and I think it's time! As the hands on the clock move, so does my baby boy's arrival. As we rush to the hospital, both excitement and nervousness collide. On Friday, June 15, 2001, roughly around 9 pm Juvon is welcomed into the world. He is embraced by a warm and loving family. As I hold him in my arms, I can't help but marvel at his beautiful brown eyes. At that moment, I know that there is no greater love than the love of my Father. I'm truly blessed and grateful that God has answered my prayers. My son quickly becomes the center of my universe. Despite the ongoing grief from losing Junior, I know I have to be strong for Juvon. He has brought life back into my world. Watching him grow and discover the world around him captivates my mind. My heart has been filled with joy and a sense of renewed faith.

When I see Juvon, I am reminded that there is still room in my heart for love and happiness. But even with all the beautiful moments, I am hit with another bombshell. I haven't even been able to breathe. In October of 2001, I find myself jobless and without a source of income. But I think there could be a solution to my problem. I devise a great plan and decide to explore stripping. After weeks of applying, I'm hired at a club. And here I am, at the age of eighteen being introduced into a world I've never seen possible before. How hard could this be? I embrace this new endeavor in hopes of making good money. On my first day, I find it difficult to take my clothes off in front of strangers. I love to dance and thought this would be easy. To ease my nerves, I decide to take a few shots of liquor. Doing so I hope to loosen up and make me more confident on stage. As I start to warm up to things my fear and nervousness disappear. The money is good but dancing is the funnest part. I started seeing so many things I never imagined for myself.

I need to keep a clear head to stay sane. If you're not careful you can be pushed into doing things you may never recover from in this industry. There are things like sex, drugs, and alcohol that are extremely tempting. With the temptation right at my reach, the drinking intensifies more and more every day. I start fighting with Rick and things get worse at home. The last thing I want to do is break up our home. Seeing myself in this predicament is so difficult to endeavor. Up until now, I've kept the demons I fight against a secret. My whole life I've been trying to cope with my mental issues. Smoking weed has helped for many years, but after I started having kids the taste no longer becomes appealing. The paranoia and anxiety have intensified so I cut back on smoking. Drinking seems to be helping numb the pain and it becomes my temporary fix from reality. Dancing triggers my drinking, but I tell myself that I can handle this and I won't get addicted. I've just been itching to escape the harsh reality of constant disappointment. As a result, drinking has become a way for me to cope. I'm a complete wreck so maybe this lifestyle can bring me some happiness.

    Disobedience to God has led me to this situation and I run every time things get hard. Running has always been deemed to be a problem in my past so why do I want to run now? Is it my selfish pride or my fear of not knowing? All that God wants for me is to be at peace and to have joy inside. But until I see this, I will continue to face unnecessary heartache and pain. Due to my selfish pride, I choose to do what I want instead of what God wants. Drinking makes me feel alive and numbs my pain even if it is temporary. I can forget all about my worries. However, this poison is harming me and everyone around me. My bitterness has built such a tall wall around my heart that breaking it away may be impossible. I've been trying to build a life for myself, but this lifestyle is beginning to ruin everything.

We can dream our entire lives for something, but when we get it, we have no idea how it's to be maintained. Sometimes I wish I could go back in time and start over, but there is no time machine for life.

Deep down in my heart, I know that I'm not making good choices. But I can't see past all the pain that I have endured all these years. Learning to forgive myself and leaving the past behind is extremely hard. With every turn I make, I keep looking back. Living in the past has been a very hard thing for me to overcome. My addiction to drinking starts to bring me more burdensome issues. My anxiety and the fear of dying grow stronger with each passing day. As I sink deeper my life continues to deteriorate. The stripper life has brought me even more pain. The shame I experience here in this line of work only adds to all the other matters of my heart. My world is spinning out of control, and I've become blind to my surroundings. Dancing has never been a permanent job. So I begin to dive into other solutions. Coming to understand that I need to reevaluate my situation, I begin to question my future. When will things change in my life?

How will I find the courage to press on? How can I overcome my trauma and addictions? How did I get here, and when will this fight for freedom stop?

Chapter 5

Facing Life or Death

In the Spring of 2005, one quiet evening mom approaches me with an unusual pain comfort she feels. Naturally concerned for her well-being, I encourage her to see a doctor. We both hold onto the belief that it is just minor, easily treatable, and soon to be forgotten. With an appointment scheduled, we anxiously await what the future holds. On that fateful day, we entered the doctor's office filled with confidence and positivity. However, after conducting a thorough evaluation, the doctor requests that she undergo a colonoscopy. His request leaves us stunned and uncertain as we begin to worry. Once the procedure is concluded all we can do now is wait, hoping for the best outcome. After waiting for the results for over a week we are informed that she has colon cancer. I'm left speechless as questions of uncertainty grow within my heart. What does this mean? What can I do to fix this problem? A flood of burdens begin to stir within my soul. In the aftermath of her biopsy, I learn that this is stage 2 colon cancer. Knowing that we have found the problem early on, the hope of a successful outcome lurks all around. While she has to undergo chemo and radiation, we try to remain positive.

But I would be lying to say that watching her endure this has been easy. Despite my best efforts, hiding my emotions is hard and it's tearing me apart inside. But the more I pray for God's help, the more I feel His comfort. Praying hasn't been easy at times but I try my best to hold onto my faith. In hopes that He will rescue her from this terrible disease, I stand on my belief. It's been hard enough to lose a child. I don't think I can survive losing my mom too. She is the only mom I have and the thought of losing her makes me weary. Watching her face so much pain is one of the most heart-wrenching things I have ever dealt with. As a result of the treatments and doctor visits time passes quickly. So I slow down take my time and embrace every moment we share. There has been constant prayer over the past months, but now the time has come to take the test again. The medical team wants to see how she is doing and if the treatment is working. While the team monitors her progress the wait feels like an eternity.

As we patiently wait the news comes in that the cancer has been eradicated and mom is now cancer-free! Mom can finally live again! But even while mom may be feeling better, she is not out of the woods quite yet. Despite going into remission, she must remain under the care of the doctors for years to come. As soon as she reaches the two-year mark, there is a much lower chance that the cancer will reoccur. During this period, she is required to visit her doctor every month. As our faith has been tested, the fear of losing her begins to fade. In the middle of almost losing her, I have an epiphany. There is a need to make things right in regard to my childhood. There is no doubt in my mind that I need to make peace. One evening, we make plans to go eat at Joe's Crab Shack. Growing up, this place has always been one of our favorite places. There have been many shared memories here and I've cherished every single moment. This is all so emotional for me but I have to stay strong. I proceed to tell her how hurt I've been over the years because of my childhood, and how I've been affected.

    The harm Jordan inflicted upon me caused me a large amount of pain. What makes matters worse, he was never held accountable for his actions. Because of this deep pain, I lashed out in ways I never wanted to experience. I didn't feel safe around anyone anymore and dreaded being at home. The much-needed conversation leaves mom and I in tears. Once the tears dry up, mom asks me to forgive her and I humbly forgive her without any hesitation. I felt so lonely for so many years, and I needed her. But now I no longer feel the same. The weight of unforgiveness has been lifted and a sense of peace overwhelms my soul. Expressing myself to her has been the most rewarding decision. It can be challenging to understand why we suffer but as the rain falls, the grass in time will grow. Flowers bloom, and trees move again. Once again I'm able to see with clear eyes. We have experienced an amazing transformation as a result of our forgiveness. As a result, our friendship has grown into a beautiful bond. I have found peace, and God continues to restore our connection. With a much better view of life, I have a heart full of love and forgiveness, I can embrace humility.

There is no better earthly love than my mother's. She has always been there if I ever had questions about life or God. I am forever grateful to have her in my life. But with pain and happiness fighting for attention, my desire for freedom continues. Now that everything is on the table and we've made peace, it's time to move forward. One beautiful evening, the topic of college comes up in our conversation. Mom wants me to have a brighter future. After watching her sick, she becomes my inspiration. A passion for helping others has become my newfound joy. In the Spring of 2006, I decide to pursue a medical career. I am applying to Remington College, a trade school where I can advance in many skills. After patiently waiting, I receive news I have been accepted into college! This is the beginning of a new future and I can't help but be excited. With the first day of class only a few months away, I prepare as best as I can. I know that everything will work itself out. And I'm starting to see things from a different perspective. The first day of class has finally arrived and I dive into my studies.

    Even though class and lectures aren't my strong points, I find a way to adjust. With my mind focused, I stay on track and away from distractions. This achievement will be my first time completing any college. The hands on the clock have always been against me as time escaped through the glass. But now I have to keep my eyes on the journey ahead. Because of moms close encounter with death, life is more precious than ever before. So when I'm not dancing or at school, we do outdoor adventures such as fishing. The serenity I feel from fishing is unexplainable. Mom has always been able to find the best fishing hole and the one in Sugar Land Texas is plentiful with bass. Usually, we make it a priority to watch the weather before heading out. But on this one specific day, we forget. What begins with the sun shining bright in the sky quickly turns into darkness. As the dark clouds form thunder strengthens in the distance. The sky grows pitch black and the rain starts falling. As I rush to gather our things, I look over and see mom sitting in her chair holding her pole. As I witness the expression on her face, I realize she won't move until she catches a fish.

When it comes to fishing, the seriousness she displays is beyond comprehension. As she sits there, drenching wet, she waits for the perfect moment. After an immense amount of patience, she catches a beautiful bass! The look on moms face is priceless. It's as if she has just won something big! This day will always be one of my many memories with mom. As the months pass, the grip I once had is gone and time slips through my fingers.

I have always tried to see the good all around me. But no matter how hard I try, I can't seem to get away from the hurt of this world. I decide to move mom in with me after her experience with cancer. I humbly take on the responsibility of providing for her. Having her close is important to me. So, I try my best to give her the support she needs. But in the summer of 2006, my whole world will be turned upside down. As I walk into the house, I hear crying coming from her room. Noticing that she is in extreme pain, I immediately call 911. As the EMT places her in the ambulance, I follow her to the hospital.

As I wait there for hours the doctors suggest I go home and get some rest. Hoping that mom will be fine, I head home for the night. Keeping a positive perspective, I hope for the best. The next morning the doctor calls me in to talk. I don't know if I am ready to hear what they have to say. But once I enter my mom's room, I feel a sense of peace. Worry takes over as I wait for the doctor. Finally, after almost an hour, the doctor comes in to inform us that the cancer has returned. The cancer is now within her abdomen and has spread to every organ. It's stage 4, an aggressive stage.

She is at a place where there is no longer treatment available. All they can do at this point is make her comfortable. The doctor explains the severity of the situation and it leaves me overwhelmed. To hear that my mother has only three to six months left is a heavy blow. I can't believe what is happening. The thought of losing her is too much to bear. Though it is difficult to accept, I take comfort in knowing that my mother's battles are known to God. I know that He understands the pain and anguish my mom is going through.

    This news is heartbreaking, and the reality of losing her is an immense burden. It's natural to feel overwhelmed and unsure of how to cope. But despite the pain, I want to cherish the time I have left with my mother. I hold onto our happy memories and make every moment count. To know that I now have limited time to share with her, I decide to pause school for a little while. I explain the situation to the school counselor and they help make my withdrawal as easy as possible. In hopes of returning once this storm passes, I hold onto the promise I made mom months ago. This news starts to take a toll on me, leading me down a treacherous path of addiction. Instead of seeking support from those around me, I turn to the embrace of alcohol and drugs. As I succumb to the temporary relief of alcohol, my consumption becomes more frequent. The need for more intensifies, pushing me further into addiction. In my desperate attempt to escape the pain, I drift toward the dangerous world of drugs. While alcohol may momentarily numb my anguish, it also robs me of joy and happiness.

The longing for genuine happiness remains, but it becomes overshadowed by the temporary respite that alcohol provides. While working at the club, a customer introduces me to a substance known as ecstasy. It presents itself as an escape from the emotions plaguing me deep down. I know that relying on drugs will only exacerbate my struggles, instead, I choose to ignore my gut feelings. Even though I need help, I choose to overlook my needs. Having to make the final funeral arrangements for mom leaves me speechless. When we found out that she only had a few months to live, mom tells me that she wants to be cremated, and tossed into the sea. At the funeral she wants us to play Al Green in celebration, not mourning. But with all this talk, I'm starting to feel the onset of grief. Mom isn't even gone yet and I begin to sense of loss. So as I take note of her request, I embrace each second we have left together. With my mind full of overwhelming thoughts, the urge for drugs arises. Turning to substances provides temporary relief, but I know they can never truly address the grief I'm experiencing. Escaping reality through drugs and alcohol offers comfort from the emotions that weigh heavily on my heart.

As I fight against the waves of uncertainty, I desperately attempt to forget the emotional torture. In doing so, I decide to find support from my family. They surround me with unwavering love and care, serving as a source of strength during these trying times. My mother, in particular, envelops me in her warm embrace, radiating love that permeates my entire being. I find a sanctuary in her arms where peace is declared over us, her children. Her love guides us through the darkest nights, illuminating our path with hope and reassurance. Her words are like a soothing balm, healing life's wounds. But just when I thought I had weathered the storm, the news I had been dreading comes crashing upon me like a tidal wave. On one Friday evening, in 2006, only three months after mom's diagnosis, I receive the news I've been dreading for months. Upon making it home to change and head to the hospice center I get a call saying that mom has passed away. At this moment, I drop to my knees and shed tears. There is nothing heavier than the loss I'm experiencing at this very minute. But I know that with her love as my guiding light, I can overcome the darkest of moments.

Despite all the preparations I've made, nothing could get my heart prepared to hear this tragic news. She has been my best friend for so long. The questions of what the future holds for me begin to creep in. What do I do now without her? Who can I go to when I have problems? Who will I be able to call when I need to talk? I'm in such pain, I can't seem to catch my breath. As I gasp for air, I try to hide my pain. But regardless of how hard I try, the devastation pulls me into isolation. The only relief I find to help the pain is ecstasy and alcohol. As a result of all the fights I have had, I don't know if I can keep going. The sudden desire to give up consumes my mind. In the midst of my desire to die, I think of my son. I'm barely holding on and I'm too weak to move ahead. The process of waking up gets harder and harder. I have never quite been able to find the right balance since Junior passed away. Here I am again as my strength is eroding with every breath. The day has come and the funeral is here.

My grief has caused me to feel a sense of loneliness and depression. But I hold on and be strong for myself and my brothers. The funeral is going just the way mom planned. Al Green is playing over the intercom and so many people are here that I haven't seen in years. Mom has a much larger family than I ever knew! It has been a bittersweet day and is coming to a close. There is something inside of me that won't allow me to give up! With a strong sense of duty, I pick up the pieces of my brokenness and keep walking. Throughout this journey, I've fought for momentum to keep going in the right direction. But whenever I start heading the right way, distractions pull and tug at my mind. After a few weeks, thoughts resurface in my mind, and I realize that my promise to mom must be fulfilled. My grades from school have been greatly impacted due to my absence. There is no doubt in my mind that with dedication and hard work, I can finish school. Although I left with a 2.0 grade average, I know that it will not be an easy task. I will need to reestablish my grades over the next six months.

I'm looking forward to getting my diploma and landing a great job one day. Not to mention making mom proud and keeping my promise. With the hope of a better future, I dive into my studies even through the difficulties. Information is crammed into each class, leaving me overwhelmed with information. As I decide to set my mind on more constructive things the vision of success keeps me motivated. By going to school, I'm turning my pain into happiness. In doing so, my mind gets much-needed contentment. I find school helps deal with my grieving process. This is not an easy time for but I know that everything will be okay. There must be a reason for all this pain in my life. All of the affliction that I struggle with has to have more meaning than this. One day hopefully, the answers will come to life. As the weeks turn into months, my past hardships and struggles lead me to complete victory. Because I've displayed perfect attendance, the school places me on the President's list. As I learn how to take blood pressure, draw blood, and give shots, things start coming together. An internship will be where I head next upon completion of my in-class training. I can put my skills to use and gain experience in the real world.

    These tools and resources will help me overcome the obstacles standing in my way. Before I even have a chance to look up, the six months have come and gone. My time here at Remington has given me the knowledge and direction to succeed. As my time here starts to end, my mind is flooded with relief. Remaining optimistic, I wonder where I'll go for my internship. Questions circle in my mind as I prepare for my final exam. It's hard to cope with the unknown, but I understand the importance of staying steady. I'm memorizing bones and learning so much in such a short time. Being faced with a significant assessment can be daunting, but I keep reminding myself to stay focused and determined. By maintaining a strong sense of discipline and resilience, I believe I can overcome any obstacles that come my way. Staying on course and continuously learning are essential steps toward achieving my goals. School has been a great step in the process of my journey. I have been able to overcome and conquer every odd that has come against me. To be here right now is not short of a miracle. I have been able to transform my 2.0 grade average into a 3.75 within six months. I know in my heart that my mom would be proud!

The need for a medical job gets closer every day. Even though I'm unsure where to go from here, hopes of getting a great job inspire me to keep moving. As my time here at school comes to a close, I decide to quit dancing. I've been waiting for the right opportunity. As I press forward, God blesses me with a cashier job at a car wash. It's only part-time for now but it will help me get through my internship. I plan to become a full-time medical assistant. It is the reason I completed the classes at Remington in the first place. Upon completion of in-class training, I'm given an internship at an Urgent Care Clinic in Stafford, TX. This place is an amazing clinic to learn allowing me to work both the front and the back office. My time here at the clinic comes with its ups and downs, but God is helping me get through. As time passes, I find myself enjoying being a medical assistant. Helping others brings so much joy. The continuous movement between my part-time job and internship makes the hands on the clock move fast. Without hesitation, I receive news that brings some much-needed relief on this journey.

As my internship at the Urgent Care Clinic winds down, questions once again arise. Who will I work for? How much money will I make? What will be my hours in my new position? But to my surprise, with only a week left at the clinic, the doctor offers me a part-time job. Even while I'm grateful, I envisioned a full-time job in the medical field. I have been hoping to obtain one full-time job in the career I went to school for. So I discuss my desire for full-time work with the doctor. He informs me that right now, all he can afford is a part-time employee. He then extends his thankfulness for all my hard work. By understanding the situation, I gladly accept his offer. I know in my heart that I'll be able to get the experience I need for my future full-time medical assistant job. For now, financially I have to keep working at the car wash. Working two jobs will not be easy but when has my life been easy? Everything is not working out the same way as I originally planned. With my mind whirling, I began to wonder if medical school was even worth the results.

But there is no turning back the hands of time. It has been almost two years since I finished school and my hope for a better opportunity is slowly fading. Every time I search for better jobs, employers request Spanish speakers. Each rejection chips away at my confidence, leaving me with uncertainty about the next steps. The optimism that once fueled my pursuit of a medical career is gradually dissipating, leaving me lost. It feels like I am trapped in a room with my back pressed against the wall. But even when all hope seems to be lost, the light starts shining through the darkness. A blessing in disguise emerges from around the corner, bringing a newfound sense of possibility. Ironically, it is not within the realm of medicine that my fortunes shift. Instead, it's in an unexpected place, the car wash. The manager here sees potential in me and takes me under his wing. He helps me see that even though I've taken a detour, there are still opportunities. With his mentorship, I regain a sense of purpose and direction. In return, I'm offered an assistant manager position. This will require full-time dedication. As I weigh my options, I know that I need to make the best possible decision.

After careful consideration, I choose the management position. The money is better and I will not have to work two jobs anymore. As I take a leap of faith, I leave the clinic. Despite my initial reservations about leaving the doctor's office, I find that the car wash offers a glimmer of sunshine. While the rejection from medical jobs may have initially felt like a setback, it opens the door to a new path. My questions are still there, hidden deep in the dark. But to find my freedom, I must continue walking. But how many more U-turns must I take? When will I let go and surrender to God? How many poor choices will it take for me to wake up? When will I step into complete freedom?

Melissa's Journey " Standing in Freedom " 142

Chapter 6

Change unfolds

Determined to heal, in 2010 I cultivate a healthier bond with my earthly father. His name is James and our relationship has always been a work in progress. After enduring the heartbreaking losses of my son and mother, I yearn to repair the fractured relationship with my father. I'm constantly being reminded on this road that nothing is ever promised. Time has never stopped for me, so why would it now? No one could have prepared me for this moment in time. No matter how hard I try, everything has always hit me at a hundred miles an hour. Not much has been said about my father, James on this walk, up until now. Our past interactions have been far from idyllic, but I know the importance of mending what has been broken. James has not served as a commendable role model drifting in and out of my life. However, I am resolved to avoid regrets and embrace every form of forgiveness. The loved ones I have lost illuminates the significance of cherishing relationships. Reflecting on the quality of my connections with those closest to me I long for restoration with my father.

While our past experiences have been marred by disappointment and inconsistency, I am approaching this with an open heart. Longing to let go of resentment and bitterness that have lingered for far too long. By extending forgiveness to my father, I am choosing to embrace our reconciliation. While understand that he may not have been the role model I so desperately needed, I am willing to acknowledge this complexity. Perhaps his struggles have hindered my ability to be a consistent presence in my life. Forgiveness is not a sign of weakness but rather an act of self-empowerment. Which in turn allows me to relinquish all my anger and resentment. As I press forward, a constant reminder of fragility emerges. Forgiveness can have a profound impact on relationships. I open my home and invite him to stay in hopes of saving our relationship. He has been homeless for quite some time so without hesitation he accepts my invitation. Wanting to make amends I engage quickly, embracing the chance to set things right. A great deal of weight has been attached to unforgiveness between us. So after dinner one evening, I decided to engage with my father. Nervousness begins to creep in as I share how I've felt since childhood. In the past, I've seen a lot of arguing and temper tantrums that have damaged my mental health.

It is even possible that I have passed on some of his characteristics to my son. I can feel the heat rising in the room while maintaining my composure. The incident involving Jordan and the lack of support from my father left me incredibly hurt. All I needed was for him to care. His inaction has deeply wounded me, contributing to my emotional turmoil. The trauma from my childhood has played a significant role in my struggles as an adult. The emotions and mental anguish that I endure have left a lasting impact on my well-being. My father must understand the extent of my hardships. Only then can he truly grasp the gravity of the situation. I extend a warm hug after reaching a point of forgiveness. Peace overwhelms me in that very instant and healing takes root in my heart. But the very next morning as I awake I find that he has vanished once again. Compelled to take action I begin searching. I worry so much for my father and his safety. As I realize that his health is deteriorating from his battle with diabetes it becomes increasingly distressing. Because of the risks associated with life on the streets, it is the last place he should be. Despite my genuine efforts to provide him with alternative solutions, he consistently chooses the uncertainty of the streets.

Various strategies to convince him to make more responsible choices have caused me great distress. Regardless of the consequences, he still chooses to walk on this path. The diabetes has taken parts of his foot, and things could get worse. No matter how hard I try there is no way to keep my father safe. And as I wonder, an unforeseen phone call comes in just days after James' disappearance. A police officer calls to explain that they found my father dead in a parking lot in downtown Houston. The weight of this dreadful news leaves me speechless. I struggle to find the right words to express the shock that floods my heart. Memories of my father flash before my eyes, and I can't help but feel overwhelmed. As my mind grasps the news, a lingering thought crosses my mind. All I care to know is that he makes peace with God. It hurts my heart deeply to know he was alone when he passed. I tried so many times to help but I couldn't force him to listen. All I wanted was for him to be safe and to get back on his feet. My father was a solitary man, lacking friends or confidants.

    Due to this, only me and my two younger brothers attended his funeral. While saying our goodbyes, we hold onto the memories. Deep down it pains me to think that he carried his loneliness to the grave. But at this moment, I am left to face the reality of this tragic event. The police call threw my world into disarray. So I must find the strength to navigate every emotion and practicalities ahead. It's a heavy burden to bear, knowing that I will never see him again but I need to be strong. As I struggle with the overwhelming grief, I find contentment in knowing that my father's pain is finally gone. Wondering if I will see him again in eternity weighs heavily on my heart. I don't quite know if he was close with the Father. Although he may not have had a network of friends, he was a part of my life. While this too shall pass, I let go of this burden and give it to God. In turn, I lean on the strength of my loved ones and my father's memories. Time has slowly disappeared and some more news hit me like a two-ton truck. One of my brothers calls to inform me that Jordan has hung himself in prison. News of Jordan's suicide is unexpected. There has been this void between us for so long.

He was the next person I needed to address. But now it's too late. His death has left me with so many unanswered questions. What led him to such a desperate act? Was it the guilt of his actions, the weight of his past transgressions? Or was it something deeper, something I may never understand? It's a difficult pill to swallow and one I'm not sure I'll fully come to terms with. My once strong stride has now transformed into a sluggish walk. With all these emotions stirring up inside I am left with the difficult choice of attending his funeral. Despite forgiving him years ago, the pain still lingers in the depths of my heart. Attending his funeral may be my final chance to have the closure I need. My excessive indulgence in drinking and drugs has only served to mask the underlying issue. With a humble heart, I embrace the last chance I have to fully let go. Anticipation and anxiety build up as the days draw closer. The support from my brothers is invaluable and brings me comfort. Thoughts of seeing him for the last time and bidding farewell stir within me sadness, regret, and even anger.

Gathering the strength to make peace with this situation removes any lingering hesitation.

The day arrives and I try my hardest to be emotionally prepared. Standing before the gathering, I am determined to speak out for forgiveness. It is not easy, but I recognize the importance of letting go of past grievances and finding closure. With a deep breath, I share my thoughts and feelings. As I stare into the casket, my heart expresses great hurt and I begin to sweat. The nervousness and sadness overwhelm me and fill me to the brim. It is a cathartic moment, releasing the burden of resentment that has weighed me down for so long. I am coming to understand the power of forgiveness and the strength it takes to choose empathy over resentment. It is a bittersweet experience, filled with liberation. Standing there, it settles in that his life is over. The weight of his actions hangs heavily in the air. Freez in silence, something changes. By releasing forgiveness to all who have wronged me I can finally be free. My heart refuses to accept hatred, yearning for something more. With a newfound sense of freedom, I unlock a key to my liberation. The bitterness that once clouded my mind dissipates, making room for wholeness. Yet, even as I let go, questions still linger in my heart. I long for answers.

The wounds run deep, and the scars may never fade. But at this moment, I acknowledge that I once hated him for his actions. I understand that this hatred served only to further entangle me in my pain. Now here I stand, looking back at a crossroads on my journey. I made the conscious decision to release the negative thoughts that have held me captive for years. As I await answers that may never come, I hold forth patience. In hopes of freeing myself from the chains of resentment, I open my heart to the power of love and compassion. On this journey, happiness will once again be found. After dealing with so many tragedies, I can use some rest mentally. The idea of taking a trip creeps into my mind. I've never really been anywhere so maybe now is the time. Exploring new places, trying new foods, and experiencing different cultures has always been appealing. However, amidst these daydreams, I can't help but feel guilt. I have lost sight of the one person who needs me the most, my son, Juvon. Just yesterday he was a little bundle of joy fit tightly in my arms. Time has moved like a tidal wave.

 The desire to make up for lost time circles around tugging at my heartstrings. Wondering why it has taken me so long to realize the importance of the present perhaps I'm starting to see it from a different perspective. Up until recently, my mind has been focused on my desires and aspirations. I'm reminded of the precious moments I have missed with Juvon. My drinking, the distraction, and drugs temporarily drifted me away from him. It's time to step back from these distractions and embrace our weekend together. As we head on an adventure, I'm embraced by Juvons. Tulsa Oklahoma is where we are headed and it will take us eight hours to reach our destination. Upon arriving in the evening we check into the hotel for rest before exploring this tranquil city. The next day, we set out to indulge in sightseeing. Immediately I'm struck by the view of Turkey Mountain and its breathtaking beauty. To make the most of our limited time here, we try and accomplish as much as possible. With so many things to do we narrow down a range of things, from great food, shopping, and outdoor activities.

But the best part of the whole trip is by far watching the sun go down at Turkey Mountain.

As the hours pass, time slips, and before we know it, it's time to head home. After an incredible weekend filled with adventure, we reluctantly want to leave. To avoid heavy traffic, we head out early. So we gather our belongings and bid farewell to Turkey Mountain. The memories made during this weekend getaway will forever be cherished. Though our time here has been short, the moments we share remain etched in our hearts. As we drive away from Tulsa a sense of fulfillment washes over me. I'm grateful for the opportunity to witness such natural beauty and immerse myself in its wonders. While we may not have seen everything, we appreciate the stunning landscapes and the serene atmosphere. Reflecting on our time spent here, we can't help but feel a tinge of sadness as we say goodbye. Nevertheless, we are left with the anticipation of future visits knowing there is still more to discover. With the road ahead, I redirect my focus to getting home safely. Two hours into the drive, we pass through a small town called Durant. I am forced to stop as we approach a red light.

While waiting for the light to change, my eyes are drawn to a truck hurtling toward us at an alarming speed.

Not wanting to disturb Juvon as he peacefully sleeps in the back seat, I begin to pray. In a split second, as the truck bore down on us, I reach out to God in need of His help. The truck collides with our car, and I feel a sudden jerk in my neck followed by a sharp pain shooting down my back. As the shock subsides and I regain my senses, I quickly assess the situation. Medical assistance is required so an ambulance is called to the scene. The gravity of the situation is apparent and medical attention is a top priority. Once the ambulance arrives, Juvon and I are taken to the hospital. We both undergo a series of tests and are examined by the doctor. They need to ensure that we have not suffered any internal injuries. After many tests are performed, we are placed in a room to await the results. Hours later, the doctor diagnoses us both with whiplashes. Emotions begin to run through me like wildfire! With doubt in my mind, I'm left with many questions. I'm unsure of where my car is or if it's drivable. How will we get home? The fact that we are stranded in an unknown place without a car makes me anxious and afraid.

    To make matters worse I think I misplaced my license and I have to be at work at eight a.m. tomorrow morning. As we sit in the waiting area I try to gather my thoughts. In search of solutions, I call around, hoping to find my car. In the midst of panic, I hear someone call my name. A police officer is standing right behind me stating that he has my license. By accident, he put it in his pocket after completing the police report. My license fell out after emptying his pockets earlier that day. During our conversation, he asks me if there is anything I need. He listens as I explain the situation to him. He goes on to tell me where my car is as my anxiety dissipates. I truly believe that God brought him to me. This whole time I've been desperately crying and praying for help. I haven't quite grasped the extreme of this situation, but I know that my faith has inevitably strengthened. A sigh of relief fills me when I reach my car and see it's driveable. There is something about this incident that stirs up a sense of calmness from within. As we retrieve my car we begin heading back home.

An unimaginable weight has been lifted, and all the heaviness from my past continues to shift. A strong desire to pray and thank God intensifies with every mile. The more I pray, the stronger my peace grows. Everything originally meant to pull me further from God is drawing me closer to Him. The whole ride home God's presence is profoundly comforting. But as we make it home, I begin feeling physical exhaustion. As I lay there and rest I am overwhelmed by God and His faithfulness. Sleep has never felt so sweet. The next morning, I contact my job explaining my pain, and requested a few days off. After a day or two of rest, I begin addressing the issues with my car. So, I set out to get my car fixed and to find a lawyer. Due to the other driver being at fault, I plead my case to the insurance company. With everything now in order I will be patient while they are at work on my case. Many months later I receive the compensation that I deserve. This whole situation left me in a very vulnerable state and I'm pleased with the results. My Father is faithful and has carried me through this trial. Now I have a large sum of money and the plan is to do right with this blessing. But the voice in my head pulls me back into my heavy addictions. All of the plans and goals I wrote down seem to be fading. Hoping to get out of debt and pay some bills becomes just a fragment of my imagination.

My drinking starts to spiral out of control again, and my drug use increases. Spending here and spending there, the money quickly disappears. Most of my settlement is wastes on cigarettes, alcohol, and ecstasy. In tunnel vision, I'm surrounded by my addictions. No matter how hard I desire to escape, distractions continue pulling me back. The more I drink, the more the tension subsides. These addictions have paved a way for me to temporarily escape reality. Even when I face self-destruction, I refuse to wake up from this terrible nightmare. I desperately want to enjoy life again, but I don't know where to start. Once again, I'm left to pick up the broken pieces of this life. While holding my head up, my current job takes center stage. Nobody knows the demons I fight behind closed doors. Every day I pick myself up, hoping that one day freedom will soon come. Almost every day I wake up with a hangover. I'm sure everyone can smell the beer on my breath.

With this mask on my face, how could anyone fully know the depth of my character? So, after one very stressful week, I decide to treat myself to dinner at Apple Bees. When I arrive, I order my food and take a seat outside. As I sit, a group of women across from my table sparks up a conversation. My mind doesn't know how but the conversation comes up regarding God. I share with the ladies how God has saved me from so many adversities. But amid our conversation, a gentleman sits down across from my table. Not aware of what is about to happen immediately I am pushed back into the fence and blackout. When I regain consciousness, my hand grasps the back of my head and is covered in blood. Dazed and confused, the impact has made me incoherent. The unexpected force catches me off guard, leaving me disoriented. In an attempt to regain my composure, my eyes meet the concerned and alarmed people in the restaurant. The onlookers quickly rush to my aid with their worried voices of concern. Gently, they guide me away from the scene and ensure my safety. Due to the bleeding, an ambulance is called to examine my head. While waiting for the EMT, the witnesses provide me with some solace, soothing the shock that courses through my veins. In this moment of vulnerability, their presence reminds me that I am not alone. As the initial shock begins to wear off, I come to understand the gravity of the situation.

The man who pushed me has already fled the scene, leaving behind a trail of confusion and unanswered questions. Upon the EMT's arrival, I am swiftly transported to the hospital. The situation's urgency is evident as I require stitches. However, medical professionals must assess the internal condition of my head to ensure there are no further complications. The medical staff examine my head to ensure there are no injuries that could pose future risks. Upon completing the test on my head the medical team find that there are no issues to cause for alarm. After I receive treatment I am discharged. They provide specific instructions on how to take care of myself at home. Although my time at the hospital is brief, the care and attention I receive is exceptional. I safely return home, grateful for the expertise of the medical team. Though the incident may have been distressing, I can now focus on my recovery. Following the prescribed course of action. The vivid picture of that moment plays continuously in my thoughts. Wondering and questioning why this happening leaves me speechless. The moment shook me to my core, leaving me powerless. Finding comfort at home where quietness from the chaos can be restored. I pray, seeking guidance and strength from God. During these moments of prayer, God reveals to me His mercy.

With each passing second He is pulling me closer. Through God's divine intervention, He sheds light on my path. His presence brings me calm serenity amidst the storm. I am reminded that, even in the darkest times, God's light can shine through. In time, bringing contentment to my wounded spirit. As I strive to find rest and rejuvenation, God's presence provides peace to my heart. In Him, I find the strength to face each day with renewed hope and resilience. Moving forward I seek to put the past behind me. A desperate need to have some fun comes to the surface. A few weekends after my assault, I head to Galveston, Texas. I love the water and beauty at the beach. As both Juvon and I find some peace, the itinerary for our trip takes shape. Our first day in Galveston is spent exploring local attractions. A weekend spent by the beach, absorbing the sun feels like a picture-perfect movie. We visit the historic Pleasure Pier, where we enjoy thrilling rides and breathtaking views of the Gulf of Mexico. The vibrant atmosphere and laughter fill the air, instantly easing the weight on my shoulders. We also stroll along the Seawall, admiring the ocean's vastness and feeling the gentle breeze against our skin. On the second day, we indulge in water activities and venture out into Galveston Bay. As we glide through the water, I feel a sense of joy I haven't felt in a long time. In the evening, we find a cozy spot on the beach engrossed in the breathtaking colors painted across the sky. As the weekend ends, I see that this trip has allowed me to escape the darkness.

    The sound of crashing waves and the warmth of the sun on my skin rejuvenate my soul. Galveston has become a symbol of resilience and a reminder that there is beauty and peace even in the darkest of times. An overwhelming sense of gratitude washes over me as we prepare to leave. The natural splendor of the beach will hold a special place in my heart. Even in the face of adversity, there is always a chance for happiness. No matter how hard I try to ignore my addictions, something always comes to tear down my progress. In my relentless struggle against temptations, it becomes evident that my addictions still hold a firm grip. Despite my best efforts, I succumb to its power time and time again. The battle for self-control is arduous, and I lack the sound judgment that is necessary. The weight of these challenges can be overwhelming. Often my alcohol and drug needs casts a shadow over every aspect of my life. Once again, darkness engulfs me, leaving me isolated and helpless. I'm trapped in a vicious cycle with a desperate need to break free from my weaknesses. Having fun and enjoying life has always come in small spurts.

    No matter how hard I try to fight back, it seems as if a heavy weight pushes back. It is disheartening to witness the continuous unraveling of my efforts. While watching the walls I've built crumble right before my eyes. The lack of stability and constant setbacks deepen my despair. Every step forward is followed by two steps back, leaving me trapped in a perpetual cycle of self-doubt. In this state of vulnerability, I find myself questioning my strength and resilience. How can I hope to overcome the clutches of addiction when it has an unyielding hold on me? The road ahead appears bleak and uncertain, filled with obstacles that threaten to derail my progress. But even then a tiny flicker of hope remains. Despite the overwhelming odds stacked against me, I refuse to surrender. With determination, I hope to gain the strength to break free from the chains that have me bound. Alcohol can influence my decision-making abilities which leads me to make irrational choices. Despite the warning signs, I ignore the opportunity to run from mistakes. One in particular that occurs far too frequently is drinking and driving. This decision has become a daily ritual and is getting out of control. When I drink there are often that I feel untouchable. It's a dangerous habit that jeopardizes not only my safety but also the safety of others. Drinking alcohol gives me a peculiar effect. It makes me feel invincible, and it is a dangerous road to travel. In this state, I often let my inhibitions run wild.

Deep down I know it's a matter of time before this reckless behavior comes to a halt. Despite ample warnings to stay home, I head out into the unknown. The beers I've already drank haven't given me a big enough buzz so I stop at the store and grab three more. About an hour later, I arrive on the outskirts of Katy, and the once tipsy feeling transforms into drunkenness. I forget what drifted me into Katy as my car glides into the dark city limits. My memory has become so blurred from consuming too many beers. By this time I had drunk more than eight tall boys. Honestly, it could be more but I've lost count. I desperately need to get a grip on reality. The temporary release from the pain causes me to drink irresponsibly. The problem is so much deeper than the drinking. Until I get a grip on my addiction the slipping will continue. Seconds later I turn around and head back towards Houston. My home is roughly about thirty minutes from where I'm located at this very instant. The freeway is not going to be my route home tonight. So I make the somewhat conscious decision to take back roads. As I cross into the intersection I swerve, causing me to hit the curb. But I continue driving not aware that my tire has blown.

Moments later, the tire pressure light comes on. It's difficult to see clearly because the alcohol gives me tunnel vision. Making rational decisions is not my strong point, especially while intoxicated. If things can't get any further deteriorated, the back wheel starts forming sparks. Normally, most people would have pulled over as soon as they noticed a flat tire, but I didn't. But my only mission is to make it back home. Everything else surrounding me is irrelevant. But now I've caught the attention of a police officer. Not only does he pull me over but now I may be arrested. At this point, I am numb and ready to submit to his authority. I have no fight left in me and my heart is heavy. I'm walking down a slippery slope full of destruction. Unaware of what lies ahead, I am given no choice but to surrender. To my surprise, however, the officer decides to do something unexpected. He insists on taking me to a sober house instead of jail. In this place, I will have to stay overnight and undergo a detoxification process. I'm too drunk to be aware of what has just occurred but te grace of God is evident.

One day, the officer's decision will make perfect sense and change my life forever. But for now, I am clueless as to how grateful I should be for his life-altering decision. As soon as I make it into the holding area, the nurse administers a breathalyzer test. My alcohol concentration is 2.0, which is a felony charge in Texas. As I sit there, the officer says, " wow, " as he looks into my eyes. Once he sees I'm safe, he leaves, never to see him again. The grace that God displays towards me through the officer is priceless. My choice should have gone another way, but God shows me mercy. I'm extremely grateful for what that officer did, but will never be able to thank him. There is never a day that passes that I don't think of what he did for me that night. Even when God should have left, He is still here holding my hand. God's thoughts are not driven by harm but by peace. It is through every wrong decision that I have made, that God's love has shined even brighter. I firmly believe that I would not have made it this far without His presence. If I were God, I probably would have given up on myself a long time ago.

But I'm not Him, His love is unwavering. I know that He sees my pain. He knows of the strong grip the drugs and alcohol have on my life. Addiction entangles my mind and body, and unless I acknowledge the problem, I will remain trapped. I'm ready to go after a long and dreadful night. Yet, the fight against my mental prison continues. My freedom is only a few steps away. But in the vast expanse of the ocean, I find myself struggling to stay afloat. The weight of my anxieties threatens to drag me to the bottom of the ocean. There is no contentment within my mind, only a battle against the forces wanting to overtake my soul. Doubt looms larger than my faith so making it out alive is nothing short of a miracle. But even now, God is faithful and continues to protect me. But why? All I can do is add this to the many questions. In hopes of finding freedom, the answers to my solutions grow dimmer by the second. How much more will it take for me to listen? Why can't I see what is happening? How will I be able to free myself from these addictions?

Melissa's Journey " Standing in Freedom " 168

Chapter 7

My encounter with demons

In June 2018, I seek to break free from the cycle of monotony. I've been in the same apartment for eleven years, and so many painful memories reside within these walls. Many of which will never be erased from my mind. In my wildest imagination, I never thought my son would be entangled in a dark and demonic world. At the age of nine, he stumbles upon something that will forever change our lives. Little did I know that a seemingly innocent day of outdoor play would lead him to the forbidden realm of the Ouija Board. Adorned with letters and symbols, this seemingly harmless board held an ominous secret. The Ouija Board, known for its ability to connect the living to the spirit world, had unwittingly become a part of my son's innocent playtime. The dangers of his actions cause significant issues at home. For several days, I remain unaware of the consequences stemming from his involvement in this evil game. However, one evening, as he prepares to go to bed, I notice something disturbing on his wrist. It becomes apparent that he has been cutting himself. This revelation exposes a much deeper problem. As he opens up to me, he shares his encounter with demonic spirits associated with the game. He explains how these malevolent beings urge him to harm me, even to the point of murder.

    This news shakes me to my core. His interaction with this game has led him down a dark and dangerous path which shouldn't be underestimated. Not only has his mental and emotional well-being been severely affected, but our entire household has been thrown into turmoil. My footsteps echo through the halls as I walk through the house, carrying the weight of anxiety. As I pace back and forth, my prayers flow continuously, seeking solace and guidance amid uncertainty. I expect that everything will be better and my child will be free from the shadows that have crept into his life. Juvon is a wonderful child and innocent. Yet, he has stumbled upon the wrong games, veering off the right path. With resolute determination, I demand that he never plays those games again. Understanding dawns on him and promises to abstain from the demonic Oijjai board. We find solace in a shared commitment to move forward, to protect him from the pitfalls of the demonic spiritual realm. Each night I kneel beside his bed as the moon rises, casting its gentle glow upon us. My hands tremble as I offer up prayers of protection. I beseech the Almighty, asking Him to watch over my child and shield us from the perils that may lie ahead. I pour out my love and devotion, seeking strength knowing I am not alone on this journey.

    To achieve change for us both, I take the initiative. My consumption of drugs and alcohol may be to blame for my son's demonic occurrence. It's been so hard to keep track of his needs because I've been so consumed with my world. In a renewed sense of determination, I pick up a green sheet and begin looking for an apartment. The process can be daunting, but with patience, I will find the right apartment. My commitment is to stay focused as I diligently search through listings. The weeks turn into months as I search diligently for the right place to call home. A place that catches my eye after what feels like an eternity. A sense of tranquility washes over me as I walk into the townhome. The space is inviting with its warm colors and cozy atmosphere.

The walls seem to hold promising memories. As I explore each room, my mind envisions the possibilities ahead while a sense of excitement fills my heart. This place has the potential to become a space where I can make new meaningful memories. The natural light streaming through the windows and the gentle breeze rustling through the trees outside also bring a sense of serenity.

 With each passing day, my anticipation grows as I await my approval. I can already imagine the joy of unpacking my belongings, arranging them in their new places, and making this house truly feel like home. Finally, the fresh start I have been seeking is within reach. Having peace and contentment in my new townhome is essential for both Juvon and me to move forward. Although I see this as a positive decision, my escape from the past lurks around the corner. Running to a new place may help me physically, but emotionally, my scars run much deeper. Taking one step at a time, I embrace what the future holds. My job has allowed me the resources financially to obtain this beautiful place. But after being there for almost eight years I feel as if I'm losing my zeal. The weight of my responsibility is becoming increasingly burdensome, adding to the stress that I already carry. Rather than confronting the pressure head-on, I find myself concealing my weaknesses. On the outside, my skin looks tough but on the inside,

I'm crying out for help. Despite my attempts to deny it, I cannot ignore the fact that my drinking habits are beginning to escalate. My addictions have been lurking behind the door for months now. I should have learned from the warnings I've received over the years.

With a mind filled with chatter, my thinking pattern is unhealthy, and I can't stop drinking. This unhealthy coping mechanism has become a vicious cycle. Appearing to be managing well, I find myself drifting off into the depths of darkness. Once again the questions succumb to my every thought. My mind has been my enemy this whole time, but why can't I see that? Why can't I unleash this grip on my addictions? In the depths of my heart, I feel bound by invisible chains. I desperately need a key to set me free. With each passing day, self-condemnation grows heavier upon my shoulders. Rather than seeking peace by renewing my mind and following God's Word, I am driven by the unsteady waves of my emotions. Continuously drifting away from reality, I lose sight of the truth. Plagued by doubt, I'm convinced that the mistakes I've made are too numerous to be rectified. It is as if my life is an irreparable mess, beyond the possibility of being cleaned. As I confront the wreckage of my past, I can't underestimate the power of restoration. My life may appear messy, it is not beyond repair. I have to keep fighting back to gain my freedom. While escaping the agony I feel, I look at some memories of mom. Thinking of her and Junior often help bring me back down to sanity.

Even though I wasn't able to share many memories with Junior, I think of what kind of person he would have been. Thinking of my mom brings a different reaction to my heart. As I reminisce, this wonderful memory of making candles starts a spark. We made some a few years before her passing, but only for fun. We did it together as a hobby and only vaguely discussed trying to make it a business. As I stumble upon candle-making books my heart fills with happiness. With the decision to make candles, I dive into the art. I spend countless hours experimenting with different scents and colors. The process of melting the wax, adding fragrance oils, and pouring them into molds is not only therapeutic but also a great way for me to unwind. With each step, I get closer to mastering my skills. But time after time, what seems like a success often turns into a disappointment. Time after time my progress only leads to failure. But refusing to give up, I persevere in learning the ins and outs of the candle-making process. But the cycle of excuses has a powerful hold on me, compelling me to rely more and more on drugs.

This dependency not only affects my mental and physical health but also disrupts my sleep patterns. The combination of drug abuse, candle-making, and work has led to an increase in my need for sleep. Despite my best efforts to juggle these responsibilities, I find myself overwhelmingly exhausted. However, there's comfort in my newfound talent for making candles. It has become my new adventure, providing me with purpose and fulfillment. Exploring ways to sell my product I hope that this will turn into a source of income. Each step I take on this entrepreneurial journey allows me to regain a sense of mental control. Patience hasn't always been my strong point, but I understand the need to master the skill. I must follow through even when faced with situations that test my endurance. For far too long, I have ignored God's wise counsel and allowed my desires and ambitions to cloud my judgment. Many times this has led me astray from His plan for my life. But I cannot blame anyone else but myself for my lack of obedience. I am responsible for aligning my actions with His teachings and seeking His guidance. This time, I yearn for a different outcome that leads me toward a healthier place.

Deep within my heart, I know that surrendering control to God is essential. Meanwhile, the pressures of my job weigh heavily on me, bringing my professional chapter to a close. The impending end of this era brings a mix of emotions, ranging from relief to apprehension. The uncertainty of the future is met with cautious optimism. Relinquishing control to God will strengthen me, releasing the shackles of doubt and fear. Wanting to find myself again, I quit my job. It was the only source of income I had so I needed to figure out my next move. One recurring vision that has captured my imagination is becoming an Uber driver. The main goal of this decision is to make my candle business more successful. This alternative career path would allow me more control over my time and resources. With more time dedicated to my candles, I can take my business to new heights. With the freedom and flexibility that Ubering provides, I have the opportunity to invest more in my candle-making skills. It offers a way to address my current dissatisfaction with life while simultaneously pursuing my dreams. Aware that there are challenges that must be tackled execution is key.

With determination, hard work, and a clear vision, I believe that this new path has the potential to transform my entire life. But no matter how foolproof I think my plan is, there is always room for error. Financial planning has always been quite a challenge. I start finding myself struggling with discipline. Now that I'm able to make my schedule trouble begins to rise. I've always worked for other people, so this is all new. Unfortunately, a significant portion of the money I earn from Uber is being spent on drugs and alcohol. In turn, my bills are being neglected, including the rent for my townhome. Despite living in my new home for a year now, I am on the verge of losing what I've worked so hard to rebuild. It is disheartening to see my financial stability slip away. If I just address my spending habits and make a conscious effort to curb my indulgences, maybe I can regain control. But as the days go, the bills continue to pile up. I am now left to make a few disheartening choices. As a parent, the last thing I want is to be separated from my son, but I must acknowledge the consequences of my actions. It is with a heavy heart and deep remorse that I admit to causing considerable harm to the relationships in my life.

My actions have hurt those close to me, leaving a trail of broken bonds and shattered trust. I am painfully aware of my struggles and shortcomings' negative impact on my son's life. Witnessing the consequences of my actions has undoubtedly affected him, and it is my utmost desire to shield him from any further distress. I need to address my addictions and figure out where I'm heading. So, as hard as it might be, he moves with his father, Rick. I lay in bed for days, crying all alone, hoping for things to change. Even though I smile in front of others, I'm dying inside. My whole life has been full of disappointments, and I don't see why anyone would want to be here for me. Depression has always had its hold on me, and the more I drink, the heavier it gets.

But I'm addicted to the numbness that comes with the temporary comfort of alcohol and drugs. All of the voices in my head are driving me to my knees and I can't shake them off! One evening after a very emotional day, I walk through the house crying. I'm left having to vacate my home because I no longer can afford it, and it's eating me alive.

Full of worry, I don't know where to go and I need God's help. Longing for answers, I question the things that I have always feared. In the past, I've refused His help so what will change with my present circumstances? Why would He help me now? Why will He listen to my prayers this time? His way is better than mine, and until I see that, I will always spiral further out into the deep. The feelings of fear, hopelessness, and anxiety once again consume every inch of my soul. I find myself confined to my bed, engulfed in tears. Depression begins to isolate me from reality. Days turn into nights as I yearn for a change that seems ever elusive. Though I wear a smile to mask my inner torment, inside I am withering away. Disappointments have become a recurring theme of my life, leaving me to question everything. The grip of depression is unyielding, tightening its hold on me with each passing day. In my desperation, I seek refuge in the temporary comfort that numbs the pain. Full of alcohol and ecstasy I begin to wander around the house. As I slowly pace back and forth, my eyes stare heavily into the darkness.

As I look out into the dark, I catch a view of wolf-like creatures standing on both their back feet. I'm in complete disarray. This vision looks much like what you see in the movies, but right here in my living room. An eerie silence fills the room as the air becomes tense. My heart races as I try to make sense of this surreal sight. Their eyes gleam with an otherworldly intensity, and their sharp fangs glisten in the dim light. Fear grips me, but a flicker of curiosity also ignites within. I am torn between the desire to flee and the compulsion to understand. As I run into the kitchen, I am filled with fear. To avoid overanalyzing the situation, I pray. Immediately I sense God placing me in a shield of protection. At that moment, God places me in a bubble, stopping the wolves from breaking through. I'm so left in shock I wonder if this is happening, or am I crazy? In the depths of my soul, I am certain that the vision I'm experiencing is not merely a figment of my imagination. Despite my initial doubts, I know God has granted me the privilege of witnessing this vision.

By gaining a deeper understanding of the hidden realities surrounding drugs, my eyes are opened to the spiritual realm. The impact of what I see is indescribable, and it continues to haunt my thoughts, replaying over and over throughout the night. This experience leaves me restless, unable to find peace. My thoughts repeat the profound implications of what has just transpired. Because I have seen what confirms to be evil spirits, I fear that I'm in trouble. The palpable sense of truth emanating makes it undeniable. A veil has been lifted, allowing me to peer into the dark underbelly of substance abuse. The vision reveals to me the multifaceted nature of addiction, unmasking the destructive forces that lurk behind the surface. However, it isn't until now that I experience God's undeniable power firsthand. Prayer has always been a part of my life, but up until now, I never fully grasped its significance. When I pray, I feel peace and protection beyond human understanding. God's divine presence surrounds me, enveloping me in His warm embrace. The worries and anxieties that once consumed me are replaced with calm and reassurance. Although I can't fully understand it at this moment, my faith is being strengthened in ways I never thought possible.

Even when I can't see the path ahead, I need to trust God's guidance. There is a deep knowing that there is a purpose for my existence. I am not quite sure why I have been chosen to walk this particular path, but I believe that everything happens for a reason. God's power cannot be easily explained or understood, but it is real. My experiences with substances like ecstasy pale in comparison to the profound connection I feel when communing with God. Once I calm down, I begin to feel a comforting heaviness within my soul. The next morning, I remember what happened as I reminisce about the wolves. But this time, I see them right outside my door. This vision is slightly different from what I saw the night before. God begins to reveal more. He gives me a glimpse into the world around me. God, in His infinite wisdom, has chosen to reveal to me a reality beyond what my eyes have ever beheld. In the encounter with the wolves, I witness a revelation that surpasses all others. It is through these creatures that God unveils the hidden dangers lurking outside, waiting to consume my soul. To safeguard myself from their menacing presence, I must strengthen my defenses.

Through prayer, I am learning that it is the ultimate weapon against spiritual forces. As God continues to reveal the profound depths of knowledge I need, I am noticing that wolves don't appear the same in the spiritual realm. This divine revelation is a direct response to my understanding. Wolves, as symbolic beings, hold remarkable mystical significance. They are not merely physical predators but representatives of spiritual adversaries that seek to undermine my mental well-being. The ferocity and cunning of these creatures mirror the forces that challenge my faith and integrity. It is in this spiritual realm that God has graciously shown me the true nature of these adversaries. Understanding the threat posed by these wolves, it becomes imperative to establish a defense mechanism. Prayer serves as a vital shield against their advances, allowing me to resist their influence and not fear or show panic. In prayer, I find solace, strength, and guidance. I'm able to tap into the abundant heavenly resources provided by God. This revelation is a testament to God's unwavering commitment to protection. The encounter with these wolves serves as a powerful reminder of the spiritual warfare that I face daily. Learning to pray continuously will strengthen my fight the right way. I am extremely blessed to have this opportunity.

Even though I may have been afraid for a short while, this has completely changed my prayer life. I make a vow to pray every morning before I step out of my home, no matter the reason. Now needing to face other issues I hold on tight to God's hand. But my ongoing battle with alcohol and drugs clouds my ability to plan for anything. As a result, I find myself sinking deeper into financial hardship, unsure of how to escape. I must break free from the cycle of living paycheck to paycheck. I need to find a way to secure a better future for myself. While Ubering provides me with income, I need to learn to manage and save for my future. I need to develop a budgeting strategy that allows me to allocate funds for essential expenses while also setting aside a portion for savings. By making a realistic financial plan and sticking to it, I can regain control. If I'm not already battling enough, I sink deeper into a state of laziness. The desire to avoid work becomes increasingly irresistible. The drugs keep me up all night and I have no desire to eat. Eating has become a mere afterthought.

   Even with all that God has shown me, I still choose to do ecstasy. Despite the allure of this lethargic lifestyle, the fear of homelessness hangs over me like a dark cloud. Up until now, I have been fortunate enough to have a stable place to call home. The thought of not having a roof over my head intensifies my desperation to find a solution. With the realization that I won't be able to afford the full rent amount, I have no choice but to approach my landlord. Knowing that my financial situation may not garner much sympathy, I gather the courage to explain my predicament. My situation hits home when my landlord expresses his inability to lend a helping hand. The news is disheartening, but I understand that he has his responsibilities. As I come to terms with this unfortunate outcome, I am left to explore other avenues.

In the middle of this fight, I look for videos on YouTube for encouragement. In hopes that something will lift my spirits, I desperately seek anything that may help. As I stumble across a video that has a positive message, I listen. There's something the person says that grabs me and pulls me in. He says, "Close your eyes and imagine you're on your deathbed. On your deathbed, beautiful angels are surrounding you as your soul departs from your body. These angels go on to explain all the wonderful things you could've done while on earth, but you didn't ".

Immediately begin to cry as I drop to my knees. My future has been greatly impacted by this powerful message. It allows me to search deep within my soul and question where I'm headed. I fear that if I don't overcome what has led me here, there may be no hope. This urge draws me even closer to God. In this chapter of my life, events have unfolded in a way that is both unexpected and profound. Something very unique has happened, weaving threads into the fabric of my heart. A sense of a newfound freedom looms on the horizon. It is a freedom that transcends the limitations of my issues and shortcomings. It is a freedom that can only be found in the embrace of God's loving arms. God nudges me even more to seek after Him. Because of what I've witnessed there is no doubt that God wants me close. As I start to dive into the pages of the Bible, I am met with wisdom and guidance. The words leap off the page, resonating deep within my soul. Each verse uniquely speaks to me, offering comfort, and reassurance. Through the power of prayer, God is sustaining my faith. In the midst of life's rocky terrains, I find peace in remembering that I am not alone.

With God's help, I can overcome any hardship. His strength becomes my strength, His wisdom guides my decisions, and His love sustains me. There are moments when doubt threatens to undo the progress I have made. But in those moments, I remind myself of the transformative power of believing. It is through faith that I find the courage to persevere, even when it seems uncertain. The maturation of my faith and the deepening of my relationship with God is strengthened daily. I am reminded that the only way to truly thrive in life's rocky terrains is with God's help. Why have I wasted so much precious time? Will I be able to find a place or will I have to live on the streets? When will I be able to breathe again? Why haven't I yet learned from my addictions? So I continue moving, hoping to find the answer to my questions.

Chapter 8

Fighting my way to peace

With no other viable options available, I reluctantly book a room at the Red Roof Inn on I-10 near Katy, TX. Despite my inability to imagine a better situation for myself, I have to make the best of what I have. It has become my new way of life to live day by day. As I struggle to make ends meet, I am in desperate need of a breakthrough. As a result of my lack of financial stability, I am unable to fall back on my savings. As a result, I must accept my circumstances and embrace reality. However, life has thrown unexpected challenges my way many times, and I've learned how to survive. The prospect of despair or hopelessness might seem inevitable after losing everything. Instead, I choose to see this as an opportunity for growth. As a result of this opportunity, I hope to rebuild my life from the ground up. The choice to stay hopeful overrides my current circumstances, though they are far from ideal. My limited income is only a temporary setback. To improve my situation, I will work hard and find a solution. I've been battling my addictions for over fifteen years and to see where I am breaks my heart.

Addiction is an overwhelming force that weakens me, leading me to disregard the consequences of my actions. In the midst of these difficult moments, I turn to my faith in God as a source of comfort. Throughout my journey I've come to recognize that God is the only one who can truly help. So I never lack peace, even in seemingly hopeless situations. My emotions blind me and often have a detrimental impact. This self-destructive behavior has resulted in the loss of important aspects including my mental and physical health. I acknowledge that my strength is insufficient. In my heart I know that God can provide the guidance and strength I need. By reaching out to God, I hope to find reassurance through this struggle. From being stable to homeless all within a couple of years is indescribable. For more than a decade I've yearned for freedom. I too must do my part no matter how much I pray, and seek God. Even with my heart full of doubt, questions once again arise from within. What must I do to receive God's intervention? How much more will I have to seek to find? It's impossible to deny that I am struggling. Letting go is so much easier said than done.

No matter how much I try to not think about my issues, I am afraid of what's ahead. But with the constant rollercoaster in my mind, it's hard to keep my hope alive. In my heart, I know that God is listening to my prayers and that brings me a sense of enlightenment. In times of despair, seeing that God understands my pain brings me contentment. In the midst of my addiction's intense grip, I choose to take ownership of my choices. But as soon as I let my guard down, here comes the voice of doubt. Hurtful words echo over and over again, fueling a feeling of relentless catastrophe. The constant reminders that "nobody loves you" and "everything is your fault" drown out any hope that still resides within the chambers of my heart. I know how to fight against the tide but the currents prove to be stronger. As my strength weakens I'm thrown into the lost sea. It's much easier to give in to temptation than to walk away from it all. As I buckle at my knees my flesh feels weakened. One afternoon, as I Uber, the voices of doubt arise. Restless and broken to pieces, I can't see how my life could be useful anymore. The constant replay in my head of all my past regrets has taken such a heavy toll on me.

Melissa's Journey " Standing in Freedom "

The fight I once had, seems to be exhausted without reason. Yet again, the fear of loneliness starts to plague my mind. Not having anywhere to turn, I try to find an easy escape. I've made such a mess, and there is no way that I can undo this madness. The strength required to move forward has diminished to a great extent, leaving me feeling unsure of endurance. The challenges and hardships have taken their toll, draining my energy and making it increasingly difficult to persevere. The weight of the burdens I carry seems almost unbearable, testing my limits and pushing me to the brink. It feels as though every step forward requires an immense amount of effort. The overwhelming pressure leaves me questioning whether I have anything left to give. The fatigue has settled deep within, sapping my motivation and leaving me in a state of uncertainty. The path ahead appears daunting, and the prospect of continuing seems elusive. Yet, deep within, a flicker of determination refuses to be extinguished. There is this small spark that reminds me of the resilience from within urging me to keep going. It's quite hard to explain but when I cry something happens.

Although the road may be treacherous and the journey may seem endless, strength can be found in the most unexpected places. Suicide has been a constant battle I have fought for many years. The desire to escape the complexities and hardships of life has often seemed too overwhelming to bear. But, this time, the stakes are even higher. My struggles have reached a tipping point, making it increasingly difficult to resist the idea of surrender. Yet, I understand that succumbing to these thoughts will not provide lasting peace. But even then, my mind tricks me into believing this is the only way out. One evening while driving, my mind couldn't seem to let go of the grip of disappointment. The constant tug and pull overtake me continuously. Desperately I yearn to let go of the steering wheel while driving about seventy miles an hour. An invisible force is attempting to stop me as I accelerate. Suddenly, my entire life flashes before my eyes. With each moment playing out in rapid succession a heavyweight descends upon my hands. As I come to my senses, I pull over. With tears streaming down my cheeks, I scream at the top of my lungs, " I'm tired! " As my heart races out of control, I feel a tender and warm embrace.

Within God's divine presence, a newfound stillness has taken root. All while my mind is being tortured as I sit close to the edge. I have to clear the chatter out of my head to find the neverending desire to be free! In the midst of a disastrous moment, I have come to realize the need to change my outlook on my circumstances. I have been close to death by suicide before but not like this. I thank God for pulling me out of that dark moment for the rest of the night. It wouldn't have been possible for me to be alive right now if it hadn't been for Him. So I pick my head up and overlook the almost deadly situation. The next day, something happens and I no longer want to live the way I am. Being in a hotel is not like having my place and I crave the warmth of my own home. Due to my lack of responsibility, I have found myself in this situation. After reaching this breaking point, I contact Rick for help. It's tough for me to ask for help but I put my pride aside. The two of us begin talking, and I explain what has been happening.

He tells me he wants to help and offers me a place to stay for a while. I humbly accept and am grateful to be leaving this hotel. But while I stay with him temporarily, I decide to complete an application for an apartment there. After a thorough application process, my request has been granted, and I am eager to begin this new chapter. The wishy-washy emotions are slowly disappearing. It feels good to have stability again. Almost immediately after I moved in, I noticed that things were looking up. By preparing my mind mentally the plan is to stop drinking or doing drugs. Things are also looking up finally with Uber. My apartment is becoming a sanctuary of peace and comfort, a place where I can feel at home again. I've worked hard to create a comfortable and welcoming space. But lately, something has begun to shift. I'm treading water, desperately trying to keep my head above the surface. You see, I have fear. A fear of ending up back on the streets, where I once found myself lost and vulnerable. It was a dark time in my life, a time I never want to revisit. So, I strive to do everything in my power to ensure that I never find myself in that situation again.

But as I struggle to stay afloat, something unexpected happens. My depression, like a heavy fog, creeps in. Every time my depression creeps in, I drown so heavily in its symptoms.

Isolation and hopelessness make me not want to leave home, pulling me back into familiar darkness. The weight of my depression becomes heavier with each passing day. The thought of stepping outside becomes daunting. Overwhelming emotions fill my mind with unpredictable challenges. It's easier to retreat into the safety of my apartment, where I can control my environment and shield myself from the outside world. But deep down, isolating myself is not the answer. I force myself to take small steps, to challenge the grip of depression. Trying to shake depression is hard when it goes into overdrive. I fight as hard as possible but nothing seems to be working. Even in these dark moments, isolating myself only leads to worse situations. I have only been in my apartment for six months, and already the bills are falling behind. It's a familiar scenario, one I thought I left behind in 2018. To make matters worse, now I'm in a predicament I never wanted to be in again. Frustration consumes me and the fear of being homeless once again retreats.

    Instead of seeking healthy help, I turn to my addictions. These self-destructive addictions only lead me into a downward spiral. The consequences of my actions are evident, sleeping for extended periods, sometimes two to three days at a time. It's dangerous when I add drugs and alcohol to my issues with depression. This excessive sleep pattern, coupled with my drug habit, exacerbates my despair. Unfortunately, just as I begin to wake up from my self-induced slumber, I am confronted with shattering news. Neglecting my financial obligations only adds to my burden, thus intensifying my guilt and despair. Considering my actions, I am increasingly tempted to give up. This seems like the easiest way out of this seemingly endless cycle. Instead of working to pay rent, I've prioritized my indulgences into getting high. This decision has led to a precarious situation with my apartment. However, the manager grants me a reprieve by extending the deadline for my rent by seven days. Within this timeframe, I must come up with eight hundred and fifty dollars. Left feeling overwhelmed, I'm unable to identify a way out of this predicament. There's no way I can come up with all that money in such a short time. The looming threat of a broken lease prompts me to walk away from the rental property.

Left with a broken lease, things are about to get even harder. So, I am thinking about enrolling in a truck driving school. Hoping for a more steady income and a chance to rebuild my life. My addictions and financial stress have become overwhelming, and this may be the solution to my problems. But to take this next step, I have to take a hair test. It's mandatory to pass a hair follicle test before they will accept your application. So I have devised a plan that requires I stay clean for at least three months. Maybe if I have a goal set in place to quit drugs then it may work this time. This plan is my most favorable chance of success, and I am determined to see it through. To fully commit to my decision, I make several significant changes in my life. In November 2019, I take the bold step of moving out and putting my belongings in storage. This allows me to create a clean and focused environment for myself. After discussing my situation with Rick, he offers me a place to stay. Now all I have to do is stay focused for three months. It won't be easy, but I will put in the effort. Every day I remind myself of the importance of this goal and the benefits it will bring. By staying sober for three months, I can achieve my objective and go to Truck Driving School. It will require a steadfast commitment, but I am ready to face this challenge. Once I complete these three months, I know that I will be well on my way to a brighter future. This plan is not just about passing a hair test; it is also about taking control of my life and making positive changes.

My whole life has been such a mess and I just want things to change, so I prioritize my sobriety. By abstaining from drugs for an entire week, I am convinced that I have a real chance of becoming a better version of myself. I am on the path to attending a truck driving school, which may hold the keys to my future. Since I distanced myself from drugs, I have noticed a significant improvement in my prayer life. While it hasn't been without its challenges, I keep going. I want a better life, and this opportunity feels like the perfect stepping stone. I lean heavily on God by reading the Word, and it brings about an unusual experience. Scriptures capture my heart as I continue to read. In moments of prayer, I ask God to speak to me. While seeking God's guidance, the page lands on Revelation 20:12. As I read this scripture, my eyes are transformed into a magnifying glass, allowing me to see the words in a new light. One word, in particular, stands out to me: The word, "Great" leaps off the page, and demands my attention. In that instant, I feel compelled to stop and take a deep breath. It's as if I have tapped into my true essence. Every encounter throughout my life has led me to this moment.

God has been revealing Himself to me over time. This revelation grants me a newfound understanding and is unlike anything I have ever experienced. Many others may not comprehend the revelation behind this profound impact. But I cannot overlook or dismiss this revelation. It has left an indelible mark on my soul. It opens my eyes to the endless possibilities that lie within me. I now realize that I am capable of achieving greatness and making a lasting impact on the world. Something about that moment put a level of confidence within my heart that has brought change. Even after all the effort I have put in and all the running I have done, I am amazed that God still calls me great. It is at this moment that a wave of unconditional love washes over me. God, the One who has every reason to walk away from me loves me and that profoundly overwhelms my heart.

As I immerse myself in the scripture, my passion and longing to experience more of His presence grow stronger. The words on the pages ignite a fire within me, shaping a deeper desire to know Him more intimately. It is a transformative experience, one that solidifies my commitment to seeking Him in everything.

Just look at me. I am a homeless alcoholic and drug addict who has made such a mess with my life. But even when my mess is visible, God's beauty revives my heart. Physically it seems as if I have nothing left, but to gain a deeper connection with my Father is worth more than any struggles I've endured. Since the beginning, I have been yearning for this. Despite the tools God has given me to fight against my mind, I often lose sight of Him. No matter how hard I try, It's difficult to let go of my past and it's often tormenting. However, if I keep my mind focused on change, things will work themselves out eventually. As the weeks pass, the strength to stay sober diminishes. Thoughts of worthlessness play over and over in my head. Disappointment sends waves of despair through my veins. Feeling lost with nowhere to turn, I drown in endless tears. At this moment, I decide to seek solace in the virtual realm and open my Facebook page. As I scroll through my news feed, a post from a believer catches my attention. Intrigued by the sudden desire for comfort, I listen. Despite the haze of confusion clouding my mind, his words cut through the fog with the utmost clarity. He utters a simple yet profound message, "Let go and trust God." In that instant, his words penetrate my very being, resonating deep within.

    Overwhelmed by my emotions, in that very second, I break down. In this vulnerable moment, this believer's message struck a chord. It reminds me to release my burdens and place my faith in God. A sense of relief washes over me as tears flow as if a weight has been lifted from my weary shoulders. As I listen, it becomes a source of strength, encouraging me to let go of my worries and fears. In this state, I am reminded of the power of words and how it can heal my soul. After that moment, I put my foot down and make the closet my place of worship. It's the perfect place to grow and listen to God's instruction. Seeking answers, I dig deeper into His Word. As my time in the prayer closet intensifies, so does my desire to distance myself from everything and everyone around me.

As I read, my heart yearns to do right by God. The bond that is being strengthened between me and God is indescribable. The decision to designate my closet as a place of worship is a symbolic act of devotion. Within the confines of this small space, I can focus my attention solely on Him and His teachings. As I immerse myself in His Word, I find peace. It becomes clear and resonates deeply within me when He gives me instructions. As I delve into the sacred text in search of answers, I uncover new insights and revelations.

Each passage I read brings me closer to understanding His will and purpose for my life. Spending more time in the prayer closet has a profound effect on me. The more I devote myself to this spiritual practice, the stronger my desire to detach from outside distractions becomes. I yearn for solitude, craving a space where I can truly connect with God without interruptions or interference. My commitment to living a life aligned with His teachings grows. I feel a sense of responsibility to do right by Him and to honor Him. My love for Him gets stronger and the intimacy level between us increases. The more time I spend in the prayer closet, the clearer my path becomes. My confidence rises higher than ever before. As I distance myself from the noise and distractions of the world, I draw closer to God, and He draws closer to me. Trying to break free from a sinful and fleshly way of life is undeniably challenging. The more I seek to do what is right, the stronger the attacks. Nevertheless, I choose to change and wholeheartedly pursue obedience to God. His plans for me are far superior to anything else I could ever need or want. As I embrace the new depths of my faith, I have been blessed with a newfound vision. This vision encourages me to start a diary. But not just one diary, two diaries. One that reflects my daily walk and the other to help me fight against my mental struggles. This idea truly intrigues me, as I believe it has the potential to help me address my struggles. With high hopes that these diaries will be a place where I can pour out my heart and find relief in my mind.

Through the act of writing, I hope to get a better understanding of myself. I aim to recognize patterns, identify triggers, and discover potential solutions to all my heart-wrenching issues. Writing in these diaries allows me to confront my battles head-on. They serve as a tangible reminder of my personal growth and transformation. They are a testament to my resilience, determination, and the power of God's Word. In times of darkness, I will witness my progress. There are days when the battles can seem insurmountable. Also, there are times the weight of my circumstances can feel overbearing. However, I firmly believe that these diaries will be my guide, illuminating my path toward freedom. By adopting a positive mindset and embracing the power of writing, I am confident that I will conquer my fears. By seeking God's guidance and pouring my heart onto these pages, I am taking control of my narrative. Kicking against the pricks of life, I fight back against everything that has me in a chokehold. The weight of my struggles has become unbearable, and even suffocating. In these desperate moments, I turn to the only source of solace I know my faith in God. With a heavy heart, I pray earnestly for deliverance from the mental bondage that plagues me.

    In this place of vulnerability, I find the strength to take a leap of faith. Determined to break free from the shackles that have bound me, I devise a plan. It is a simple yet profound step towards reclaiming my life. As I step out on my quest, something remarkable unfolds. The mere act of putting pen to paper breathes life into my thoughts and emotions. The words on the pages come alive, capturing the essence of my experiences, hopes, and dreams. Each day, I pour my heart and soul into this newfound assignment. It becomes more than just a simple task; it becomes a lifeline. These diaries become a sacred space where I can find comfort in God. With each entry, I go deeper into the recesses of my mind, unearthing buried emotions and confronting long-held pain. They become a means to untangle the web of thoughts that have held me captive. All while I discover a profound sense of release. The words spill onto the page, carrying with them the weight of my burdens. With each stroke of the pen, the chains that once bound me are slowly unraveling. As the days turn into weeks, my diaries become a testament to my resilience in overcoming the darkest of times.

    In this ongoing battle against my inner demons, I find peace in simplicity. I am no longer the person I once was shackled by my insecurities and doubts. In the face of my ultimate defeat, I have found the courage to fight back. With God as my guide and my diaries as my weapon, I am determined to break free. With this unwavering determination, I get the courage to reclaim my life. Everything that has been lost or stolen is being revived. I have yet to fully understand the intricate details of my journey. Throughout my history, I have yearned for a means of escape, a way to find rest for my soul. My once-cloudy perspectives are gradually becoming clearer with each passing breath. Each step I take has a significant meaning. A dark veil has been lifted, allowing me to see my purpose with a new sense of clarity. God's guidance strengthens my understanding and convicts me on how I should navigate this path of transformation. This includes not only the positive emotions that fuel my determination and resilience but also the negative ones. It is a testament to God's unwavering love that has led me to this place. Over the years, I have allowed my emotions to consume me, and overgrown out of control.

But now, I am determined to turn things around and achieve better results. The key to success lies in my consistency and refusal to give up. It has not been an easy battle, but with every setback, I find the strength to keep pushing forward. To aid in this fight, I seek answers through scriptures. The wisdom found within these sacred texts inspires me. With one diary being my thoughts and emotions, the second diary brings my mind rest. For the second diary, my first step is to gather the emotions I've faced and write them down at the top of each page. Anxiety, fear, and even depression all have a place in my diary. To contrast these emotions, I research three to four scriptures that relate to them. As I scroll through the pages, my emotions and God's Word fill the pages from A to Z. It is my goal to write at least one emotion per day, one page at a time. With each day and every word, I'm that much closer to freedom. With every scripture I write, I feel a renewed sense of purpose. I see the profound impact of renewing my mind with scripture. It is a constant process of counter-attacking each thought that creeps in, a relentless tug of war leaving me drained.

But despite this exhaustion, I continue. I simply cannot bear all these years of misery anymore. To experience true transformation, my entire life needs to be retrained by the power of God's Word. Its purity and wisdom is healing me minute by minute. Each word, each verse, carries the potential to change my mindset, attitudes, and actions. But this process is not without its challenges. The battle continues with each passing minute. Thoughts that do not align with God's truth infiltrate my mind, distracting and discouraging me. Yet I stand firm, clinging to God's promises, and allow His Word to guide my thoughts and actions. Deep down I know the reward will be worth it all. The transformation that comes from aligning my mind with God's Word is life-changing. As I immerse myself in scripture, I renew my mind, and my heart is transformed. My eyes are opened to God's love and His plans for my life. I'm constantly reminded of His faithfulness. While reassuring me that I am never alone and His presence is always here.

God's Word is reshaping my mind, restoring my soul, and leading me on a path of righteousness. As I allow His Word to penetrate my heart, I am filled with unexplainable joy. I am determined to let it permeate every aspect of my life. With each step forward, I draw closer to God's abundance. Being able to counteract my negative thoughts with God's Word is directing me and breaking every chain that holds me down. These diaries have been my tools for freedom all along and I'm so grateful. I can't fathom how much I've overcome on this journey to freedom. I have always known in my heart that there is more for me out here in the world. The desire for freedom has led me down a promising path. There are moments of doubt and triumph, but I remain steadfast in my commitment to fighting back. Setbacks are a natural part of the process, and I refuse to let them deter me from the goal. Regaining control of my mind is ongoing, and it requires patience and perseverance. Staying consistent and not giving up, I will overcome the negative forces that plague me. My recipe for success in regaining control of my mind is simple yet powerful. By refusing to let my emotions consume me, positive results will emerge. I have believed so many lies throughout the years. I'm tired of being miserable and bitter. But who said this would be easy? Nothing in life has ever been easy. Each day feels like a struggle as if I'm fighting against an invisible force.

But as I look at my diaries, I'm able to see how far I have come. They serve as a reminder that I can overcome obstacles, even when it seems impossible. There have been moments when I wanted to give up, to succumb to the weight of it all, but I keep pushing through. Two weeks pass and the mental fight draws me to my knees. I replay scripture in my mind over again. I suffocate all the lies with God's Word. A few days later, things seem different. The weight that once burdened me has been lifted and my mind is replaced with a refreshing quietness. It is as if a storm has passed, leaving behind a sense of calm and clarity. In this newfound peace, I see the beauty behind the struggles. Every hardship shapes me into a stronger, more resilient person. They are forcing me to confront my fears and break free from the limitations I have placed upon myself. But the most challenging battle I face is my constant dependency on drugs and alcohol. The grip they have on me is relentless and the fight to overcome them is a daily task. However, alongside my battle with substance abuse, I also combat addiction to cigarettes.

The struggle to break free from nicotine chains is no different from my battle with drugs and alcohol. Cigarettes hold me tightly and breaking free requires tremendous effort and determination. Because of this struggle, I realize that now may not be the best time to go to Truck Driving School. I need to focus on my walk with God and seek for my deliverance. If I don't tackle the issues I face, there may not be room for better things to come. I now see that God is my only hope. While the road may be difficult, and the mental exhaustion may be overwhelming, I continue to walk. I embrace the lessons learned, the moments of triumph, and the resilience that lies deep within. Even in the darkest of times, there is a spark that keeps me moving in the right direction. It is in this hope that I find the strength to continue living. Many questions resurface as I gain more mental clarity. Could this finally be my way out? Will I keep growing or fall back into distractions? Am I finally going to stand in the freedom that I so desperately long for?

Melissa's Journey " Standing in Freedom " 216

Chapter 9

Standing in Freedom

Melissa's Journey " Standing in Freedom " 218

In 2020, as the new year approaches, I reflect on the year ahead. It is often said that new beginnings bring new opportunities. I sincerely pray that this will be better than the past. While it is easier said than done, I am determined to face whatever lies ahead. In these early days of the year, my mind is filled with a myriad of thoughts that are difficult to put into words. There is a sense of wonder that I cannot fully express. It is as though every moment is infused with a sense of God's presence, leaving me in awe of His complex beauty. However, amidst this sense of awe, I grapple with conflicting issues. On one hand, there are the addictions that plague me, causing pain and turmoil in my life. On the other hand, there is an immense love for my Father. This battle between my addictions and His love is a constant struggle. As I enter into this new year, I am aware that the journey will prove to hold some hope. I am firm in my resolve to persevere and to grow even stronger. By taking the lessons that I've learned throughout my life, nothing can stop what is unfolding. I believe that with the support of my Father, I can make it through anything that tries to obstruct my view.

As I stand on the threshold of a new year, I pray for freedom. May this be the year that I will emerge from the shadows of my addictions? Thus, remember that even in the face of adversity, I am not alone, for I have my Father guiding my every step. For years now, I have experienced countless moments of falling, both figuratively and literally. With each stumble, I find rest in the unwavering faithfulness of God. Like a loving parent, He catches me and lifts me, allowing me to rise again. Because of His grace, I'm able to stand exactly where I am at this very moment. In the depths of my heart, I reflect on the powerful words that echo in my mind: "If God is for me, who can be against me?" These words have become my mantra, a source of strength and encouragement when faced with the trials and tribulations of life. With a resolute heart, I have made a conscious choice to change and embrace a life rooted in God. This decision requires unwavering commitment and relentless pursuit. By staying steadfast in the face of adversity, I will remain content even when the path ahead seems uncertain. It is through this unwavering pursuit of obedience that I find myself.

In a world that often seems fraught with chaos and darkness, I hold on to the belief that God's light will guide me. With each step I take, I am once again reminded that I am not alone, for God is always walking beside me. His presence gives me the courage to endure long-suffering and the confidence to face another day. Even when I stumble and fall, God has always been there to catch me. As I pursue God, I am filled with gratitude, knowing that His love and grace will always reign. Everything is shifting, and the table is being turned in my favor. If I could see what God is doing in the unknown, my mind would be blown away. Even when I haven't been able to see, I sense Him making a way. My struggles with drugs and alcohol have been significant, my battle with cigarettes has proven to be the most arduous. Despite multiple attempts over the years to quit smoking, it has always failed. For years, I have fought tirelessly against my addiction to cigarettes. Each attempt to quit has been accompanied by relentless disappointment.

With each failed attempt, it has only been extinguished by the relentless grip of addiction. The cycle of quitting and relapsing becomes an all too familiar pattern. It often leaves me feeling defeated and trapped within the clutches of nicotine. Despite my determination and numerous strategies employed to break free, time and time again, the power of addiction proves to be stronger than my will. By recognizing my weakness, I turn to God, understanding that my strength and willpower are insufficient against nicotine. It has consumed me for far too long. Divine intervention is necessary to break free from the chains that keep me bound. Entrusting my struggles to God, I humbly admit my powerlessness and seek His guidance and support. Acknowledging that I need God's help I surrender this struggle to Him. All my life I have tried to quit the wrong way. So I place my trust in God this time. Every day I pray for Him to remove this addiction. As I light a cigarette, take a few puffs, and conviction overpowers the craving. This profound awareness of His presence urges me to put the cigarette down. It is through this act of obedience that I regain control over this sickness that has distorted my life. The power of obedience lies not only in the physical act of quitting but also in the mental and emotional strength it cultivates.

The desire to change, combined with my commitment to surrender, has propelled me forward in my journey towards a smoke-free life. But even at this moment, the fear of the unknown is lurking around. But the decision to fight keeps me rooted and grounded in God's love. Change is closer than it has ever been before. Amidst the turmoil, there is a surprising sense of happiness that envelops all around me. A weight has been fortified, and I can confront the truth head-on. This courage comes from knowledge of my lessons as I gravitate even closer to God. The tables turn in my favor, not in the sense of escaping consequences but in the sense of finding freedom. Every step I have taken has been meant to put me right here where I'm at, in this very instant. The circumstances are changing, and I can feel a sense of freedom unfolding. Even though there have been material losses and pain along the way, I now know that they hold value in shaping my growth. Through it all, God has guided me to a place of rest and tranquility. Despite the shortcomings, I continue holding onto my faith that my prayers will be answered. I know in my heart that it's just a matter of time when all of my questions will be answered.

Melissa's Journey " Standing in Freedom " 223

On February 27, 2020, I'm immersed in a profound moment of prayer for emotional release. As I lay in my prayer closet, the convictions get stronger and I capture a glimpse at God's love. It is a love that's both profound and inspiring. In a silent contemplation, my thoughts turn to Genesis, where Adam and Eve were placed in the Garden of Eden. In this paradise, there was complete harmony between humanity and God's divine wisdom. The revelation God gave to me is not only about the garden but also the consequences of disobedience. As the story unfolds, I realize that Adam and Eve had to leave God because of the sin they committed. Their act of disobedience had severe repercussions, and immediately it consumed my heart with such strong compassion. Coming to grips with this truth, I am reminded of the fragility of the human condition. It's clear that even with God's immense love, I have made choices that separated me from Him. Coming to this life-altering moment, everything weighs heavily on my heart. Yet, even in this moment of brokenness, God is still making a way. Despite my many shortcomings, God's love for me remains steadfast. It is a love that transcends every failure and offers redemption. I find peace and am deeply humbled by His love and forgiveness, even in my disobedience.

His children leaving Him must have been an incredibly painful experience. The thought of leaving Juvon behind would have been devastating and I am merely a human. For the God of all things to have His children turn from Him must have deeply broken His heart. It's at this moment that the clarity of the situation hits, and I can feel love, unlike anything I have experienced before. It is love that emanates from within, touching the deepest parts of my soul. As tears stream down my face, I call out to God, offering my deepest sympathy and compassion. I can now understand God's profound love for all of His children. He touched me so profoundly at that moment. It is a love that knows no bounds and is always present, even in heartache and separation. As I reflect on this event, my pain diminishes. It has taken me many
years to come to this crossroads, but it has been worth every second. Rejection, painful memories, and hatred have brought me to this place of peace. I'm grateful for the scars that I have endured

because they brought me closer to God. I can see now how deeply my choices are hurting Him and I need to change.

As I lay there, lost in my thoughts, a strange sensation stirs within my chest. An invisible hand has gripped my heart, pulling at it with an urgency I can't comprehend. Startled, I jolt upright, gasping for breath. It's then that a deep, resonant voice echoes from the depths of my soul. "It's time," the voice whispers urgently. "Get up now!" Confused and disoriented, I can't help but question the bizarre moment, so I ask, "Right now? It's three in the morning. I will get up and leave in the morning ". Cautiously, with my senses heightened and my heart racing, I lay back down. While I try to rest, I can't shake the feeling that something significant has just happened. Once again, the pull at my heart happens! As I sit up the voice says, " Get up now and leave! " I say. " Okay " and do just as He asks. Without hesitation, I know I have to follow this inexplicable calling. So, I wake up, shower, pack my stuff, and leave Rick's house. But as I step out the door, fear creeps in and I question leaving. Did I make the right choice? Is this the right direction? As I get in my car, I drive away.

As I drive off, memories resurface of lessons I've learned from the Bible. Passages echo in my mind on faith, trust, and perseverance. I remember the stories of those who faced hardships but kept moving forward, relying on their faith to guide them. So I choose to trust God's plan, even in this moment of uncertainty. Now as I stand here in the unknown, I wonder what lies ahead. Even though fear lingers, my faith outweighs it all. I know that as long as I keep moving, I will find my way. God has not brought me this far and I know He will not let me go. He has not stuck by my side through all this just to turn around and leave. As I reflect on my life, I am reminded of the power of prayer and the importance of surrendering to God. I am even more hopeful now that the answers to my prayers are just around the corner. I eagerly await the resolution that brings ultimate peace to my heart and mind. Satisfaction in my future outweighs all of my troublesome past. The losses I have experienced hold significant value in shaping me into all that God has called me to be. I find comfort in the restful place that God has guided me to.

So I gather myself and drive to a nearby gas station. I'm unsure of my next steps, so I turn to God for guidance. With only a few dollars in my pocket, I need to make some money. So I decide to Uber until God reveals my next move. The chaos and uncertainty surrounding me call for a distraction. By immersing myself in the task, driving others around could provide some much-needed calmness. Just as I shift my attention towards work, God's voice becomes clearer. His instructions are precise, giving me clear direction. With renewed confidence, I proceed on this new endeavor, knowing that God's wisdom will continue to lead me. Hours pass and after making some money the time comes and God shows me what to do next. He provides instructions on finding a hotel. I go to the Red Roof Inn on I-10 near Katy, where I was a couple of years back. There I can pay daily room rent. The first night, a sense of loneliness and unease fills the air. I doubt leaving Rick's house and find myself in fear of the unknown. But a short while later, God reassures me I did the right thing. Being alone and uncertain of the future, I can't help but feel a mix of emotions.

Fatigue sets in, and I reflect on the constant challenges and misfortunes that surround me. But on February 28, 2020, a significant moment occurs. I grow tired, no longer deriving pleasure from cigarettes. I make a firm decision to let go of this harmful habit for good. Everything I have been doing on this road has led me to this place. All my prayers reveal new things within my soul. That night, as I prepare myself for sleep, I take a moment to connect with God. I turn to Him, acknowledging the destructive cycle I have been trapped in, and make myself and Him a promise. I solemnly declare that the pack of cigarettes in my possession would be my last, and from tomorrow onwards, I embrace quitting for good. Over time, I have made similar vows to myself, only to succumb to the allure of smoking once again. But this time, something is different. Rather than relying solely on my willpower, I surrender this struggle to God. I know how hard quitting cigarettes has been in the past. My anxiety and fear of what tomorrow holds me in fear. But in an instant, I'm reminded that this time God will take hold.

The next morning, as the sun rises on February 29, 2020, the urge to smoke becomes so overwhelming that I long to relapse. Plots of getting another pack creep in and the strong urges almost overthrow the promise I made. But this time, I know things need to change. This is not just another attempt to quit smoking but a profound shift in my mindset. By entrusting my addiction to God, I open myself up to a source of support beyond my limitations. Acknowledging that true transformation requires more than mere determination. The urge to smoke becomes so overwhelming that I long to relapse. Just to take the edge off, my mind tells me to buy a pack. But this time, I tell myself things need to be different. Because I have tried and failed over the years, I realize that God's way is now the only answer. In the past, I have constantly run and tried to do things my way, only to find that my way always fails. My entire life has been a vicious cycle of disappointment and frustration. Whenever a craving strikes, I call upon God for support. Within the first three days, the cravings overwhelm me like a flood. The pressure intensifies, making it incredibly hard to trust in God and lean on Him.

As cravings continue, I turn to God and seek Him. After experiencing this process for the first two or three times, I see the power of surrendering. It is not an easy path to follow but I find reassurance in knowing that God is here. On day three of this continual fight, I become extremely weak. Mentally exhausted, I lay down and try to rest. As I lay there, chills overcome every inch of my body. A sudden wave of coldness washes over me, sending shivers down my spine. Immediately after the chills, I notice an odd sensation. Something is being pulled off me and a weight is being lifted from my body. Little did I know, during that moment of rest, something significant is happening. There is something waiting to be revealed, something that will change my perspective on everything. As I open my eyes, I feel a calmness that I haven't experienced before. The peace that consumes me is unexplainable. Throughout the course of my life, I've felt many emotions, but this is far greater than all of them. The mental exhaustion that plagued me has dissipated and is replaced by a sense of awareness. A fog has been lifted from my mind, allowing me to see things more clearly.

The scales have been removed from my eyes and my faith becomes more powerful. Needing to have questions answered, I continue to seek God. As I study and read the Bible, I am amazed at how God reveals things to me more in-depth. With my mind cleared of all static, I can hear God better. This amazing clarity leads me to stumble upon something truly remarkable. I am determined to understand its significance. In my quest for answers, I step upon several scriptures that provide further insight into the mystery of what has occurred. One such verse is Galatians 5:1, which states, "It is for freedom that Christ has set us free. Stand firm, then, and do not let yourselves be burdened again by a yoke of slavery." This verse reminds me that through Christ, we have been granted freedom from sin, chains, and the burdens that weigh us down. It encourages me to stand firm in this freedom and not be entangled in the bondage of worldly desires. Another scripture that sheds light on this mystery is Ephesians 3:12, which declares, "In him and through faith in him, we may approach God with freedom and confidence." This verse emphasizes the access we have to God through our faith in Christ.

I can boldly approach God, unencumbered by guilt or shame, knowing that I am welcomed into His presence with open arms. I have gained a deeper understanding of God's amazing encounters due to this newfound confidence in my relationship with Him. Romans 6:22 speaks volumes about the transformation within me. It says, "But now that you have been set free from sin and have become slaves of God, the benefit you reap leads to holiness, and the result is eternal life." This verse reminds me that as a follower of Christ, I am no longer bound by sin's chains, but am now a servant of God. The freedom I have received through Christ leads me to holiness. As I go deeper into the scriptures, God reveals even more profound truths and insights. These truths have enhanced my understanding of this amazing encounter. These scriptures have illuminated my path. This allows me to walk in confidence, knowing that I am no longer enslaved by sin. God has delivered me and set me free from all my addictions. Not just one, but all of them! No more drugs, alcohol, cigarettes, anxiety, fear, or depression. The desire to smoke, drink, or do drugs has been completely erased. I know this may seem hard to understand, but it's true!

The struggles and cravings no longer entrap my mind. All along, my past has been leading me to freedom. God's miraculous power has made me free from all that once had me chained! It's through the power of believing and the support of a loving God that I have been able to break free from the chains of my addictions. One thing I've come to understand is when you seek God, you will find Him. It is through the challenges that I can truly experience the power of God in my life. By trusting in His plan and following His guidance, I have been able to overcome it. He did for me what I or anyone else could have never done. He brought me deliverance, healing, and most of all restoration. Believing plays a crucial role in allowing God's power to be revealed. I have always had free will. It is because I never lost hope, God has transformed my brokenness into wholeness. Through faith, I can see beyond the present circumstances. I believe that God is working all things together for my good.

God's ultimate plan for me is far greater than I can imagine! This is the first time in my life I feel completely free.

The weight that has burdened me for so long has finally been lifted. My entire life has been a roller coaster ride, filled with countless highs and lows. I have encountered challenges along the way, enduring trials, and tribulations that have tested my strength and resilience. But amidst all the chaos, this newfound discovery has been well worth it all. I have found freedom that transcends physical or material constraints. This liberation has not come without its sacrifices and hardships. I have had to overcome my deepest fears, confront my weaknesses, and confront the parts of myself I am ashamed of. In my darkest moments, when I felt completely lost and disconnected, I have turned to God. His love and grace have guided me throughout this journey. He has been my constant companion, never abandoning me. Even when I fought against Him and strayed from the path, He still waited with His arms open wide. God has replaced all my burdens with His unwavering love. The chains of addiction that once bound me have been shattered, and I am now free to live a life of purpose and fulfillment. His love has opened my eyes to a world of possibilities and given me the strength to overcome any obstacle.

This newfound freedom has changed my life forever. It has allowed me to embrace life with a renewed sense of hope and joy. I am no longer weighed down by the burdens of my past. I am empowered to create a fulfilled future. This freedom is a precious gift that I will always cherish and never take for granted. He always saw the good in me, even in my lowest moments. Even with my doubt, He never wavered in His love, despite my flaws and mistakes. Reflecting on the twists and turns, the detours and cautions, I now realize that every step was bringing me closer to the lover of my soul. Each experience has shaped me into the person I am today. With each hurdle I've overcome, I have grown stronger and more resilient. I am no longer defined by my past mistakes but by the grace and forgiveness that God has bestowed upon me. It is a feeling of liberation like no other, a sense of belonging that permeates my being. As I walk, I am filled with gratitude for the One who believes in me. His unconditional support has illuminated my path. I am reminded that I am cherished and valued by the creator of all things.

With each step, I grow closer to God, the One who always sees the best in me. I am filled with thankfulness and joy, knowing that His love will continue to be my guide. God has given me a second chance to do things right. Finally, at thirty-eight years old, I have a reason to live and I have found purpose. All these years, it has been up to me to find Him! Running only prolonged my freedom. Sometimes we must come to the end of self before we will listen. I may have lost everyone and everything around me but I still have God, the One who truly matters. Every shackle and chain has fallen and I will no longer be bound by addictions! Spiritual freedom is here for all! All the answers to my questions have been revealed and I have a peace that passes all understanding. I no longer want to please man, now I only choose to please God. Every step I take now belongs to God. It's now time to love Him with all my mind heart and soul. In this moment of profound gratitude, I have been blessed with a divine presence that has transformed my life.

    The sheer magnitude of this gift is beyond words, as it has brought heaven itself into my presence. Now, I am acutely aware of the profound impact God has had on my life. Every step I take, every decision I make, and every breath I breathe acknowledges His boundless grace. Recognizing that only through God's infinite love and mercy I have been granted this freedom. His presence has lifted me from the shackles of my past, granting me the courage to forge ahead on a path of righteousness. He has always loved me wholeheartedly and now it's my time to do the same in return. It is not merely an obligation or a duty, but a deep-seated desire born out of immense gratitude. I want to devote myself to Him, to honor and glorify His name in all that I do. For the rest of my life, I will continue to stand in freedom! It only takes a small mustard seed of faith for God to do the impossible. Trials strengthen us! My journey is not over, it has only just begun! Continuing steadfast in love I will do the impossible! Setting my eyes upon the lover of my soul, I will run this race until my time here on earth is up!

To be continued.....

Written by Melissa Fisher

Visit my website: https://melissasbookstore.com

Or email me @ melissasbookstore.com

Melissa Fisher owns the rights to this manuscript

Made in the USA
Columbia, SC
28 August 2024

a lot for him. I never meant to hurt him. My marriage was falling apart and I..." Katherine stopped herself. She didn't owe Sylvia an explanation and she doubted if Sylvia would even relay the words back to Jonathan. She felt tears welling up as she once again came to the realization that she would probably never talk to him again.

Sylvia sensed Katherine's emotional struggle and gently laid her hand on her arm. "Don't worry. He forgives you. I know he does. He's not mad at you. He's never said anything negative about you."

Katherine had just nodded her head and let a single tear fall down her cheek. She wiped it with the back of her hand and bit her lip, trying to regain her composure.

"I'd better get back before he comes out here looking for me," Sylvia had said. "Take care."

Once again, Katherine just nodded and watched as the other woman made her way back down the corridor. Sylvia was almost at the jewelry store when Jonathan walked out to meet her. Katherine stayed put, frozen in place. She watched the couple as they exchanged words, then Sylvia disappeared back into the store. But Jonathan remained in place and slowly turned his head in Katherine's direction. Their eyes met and she knew he immediately recognized her, even from a distance.

Katherine tensed up, expecting Jonathan's gaze to turn cold. But it didn't. At first he looked surprised, then after a few moments ticked by, something of an understanding crossed his features. Then finally he gave the slightest nod of his head and the corners of his lips turned up. Katherine, who had been holding her breath, finally let it go in relief. She smiled at him and held up her hand, giving him a small wave, then reluctantly turned away. Instead of walking into the cooking store she found the nearest women's restroom, and once she made sure no one was in the stalls, she let herself sob.

Later that night, when she was home and the children were in bed, she let herself go over the scene in her head again. She pondered over everything that Sylvia had said. She had assured Katherine that Jonathan harbored no ill feelings toward her, and when Jonathan saw her, even though he was a good distance away, she could see it in his eyes. Sylvia had been honest. He wasn't angry with her. Katherine had the feeling that maybe, somehow, he really did forgive her.

"You ready for bed?" Nathan's voice came from their bedroom, bringing Katherine back to the present. She yelled out to him that she'd be right there, finished washing her face and walked out of the bathroom.

"Were you getting impatient waiting for me?" Katherine asked with a seductive tone as she walked toward the bed.

"Yes, as a matter of fact I was," Nathan said, his eyes taking in the new nightgown she was wearing. "Wow. Where'd you get that?"

"I bought it when I went shopping with Lauren for her honeymoon stuff. You like?" Katherine sat down next to Nathan on the edge of the bed and ran her hand down his arm.

Nathan grabbed her and pulled her close to him, "Yes, I like."

Katherine giggled and gave her husband a kiss, "Slow down, Flash. We've got all the time in the world."

Nathan kissed her back tenderly. "You're right, and I plan on making the most of it. Remember that vacation you've been hinting around about?"

"Hmmm...of course." Katherine murmured, tracing her hand across his chest.

"Well, it just so happens that my boss gave me two weeks off in June. So, it looks like I'll finally be taking you to Italy. It can be our second honeymoon."

Katherine pulled away slightly, "You have no idea how wonderful that sounds."

Nathan noted the hesitation in Katherine's voice. "Hey," he said gently and cupped her chin in his hand. "I am taking you on this trip, no matter what."

Katherine met his sincere gaze and asked, "Do you promise?"

"I promise."

THE END